FROM
READING
TO
WRITING

3

LINDA ROBINSON FELLAG

PEARSON
Longman

From Reading to Writing 3

Pearson Education, 10 Bank Street, White Plains, NY 10606

Dedication: *For Nadia and Nora with love*

Staff credits: The people who made up the *From Reading to Writing 3* team, representing editorial, production, design, and manufacturing, are Eleanor Barnes, Rosa Chapinal, Dave Dickey, Oliva Fernandez, Massimo Rubini, Loretta Steeves, Jennifer Stem, Jane Townsend, Paula Van Ells, and Patricia Wosczyk.

Text composition: ElectraGraphics, Inc.
Text font: 11 pt New Aster
Credits: See page 210.

Library of Congress Cataloging-in-Publication Data
Bonesteel, Lynn.
    From reading to writing / Lynn Bonesteel . . . [et al.].
        p. cm.
    Includes index.
    ISBN 0-13-205066-8—ISBN 0-13-612780-0—ISBN 0-13-233096-2—ISBN 0-13-158867-2 1. English language—Textbooks for foreign speakers. 2. Reading comprehension—Problems, exercises, etc. I. Title.
    PE1128.B6223 2010
    428.2'4—dc22

                                                                2009032265

ISBN-13: 978-0-13-233096-1 (with ProofWriter™)
ISBN-10: 0-13-233096-2 (with ProofWriter™)

ISBN-13: 978-0-13-247405-4 (without ProofWriter™)
ISBN-10: 0-13-247405-0 (without ProofWriter™)

PEARSON LONGMAN ON THE **WEB**

Pearsonlongman.com offers online resources for teachers and students. Access our Companion Websites, our online catalog, and our local offices around the world.

Visit us at **pearsonlongman.com**.

ISBN: 0-13-233096-2 (with ProofWriter™)   2 3 4 5 6 7 8 9 10—V016—13 12 11 10

ISBN: 0-13-247405-0 (without ProofWriter™)   1 2 3 4 5 6 7 8 9 10—V016—13 12 11 10 09

Printed in the United States of America

Contents

(continued)

Introduction

OVERVIEW OF THE SERIES

From Reading to Writing 3 is the third in a four-book series that integrates reading and writing skills and strategies for English language learners. The four-book series includes:

Book 1—Beginning Level

Book 2—High Beginning Level

Book 3—Intermediate Level

Book 4—High Intermediate Level

Reciprocal Reading/Writing Integration

From Reading to Writing provides a complete sequence of high-interest, thematically connected activities that reciprocally integrate reading and writing.

- Students build competence in vocabulary and reading as they move toward writing skill development and completion of a writing assignment.
- Students study the features and language of reading texts and learn to apply them in their own writing.
- In the same way, writing is integrated into the reading process in accordance with research that suggests writing can enhance reading comprehension (Mlynarcyzk, Spack).

STRUCTURE OF THE BOOKS

Books 1–3 contain eight thematically focused units. Each unit consists of two topically related chapters, divided into two main sections— Reading *and* Writing—which are linked by a bridge section, From Reading to Writing. Book 4 is organized into nine units. Each unit consists of two thematically connected readings that have accompanying skills and practice activities and are linked by a bridge section. Each reading is also followed by a writing section.

Books 1–3

Each chapter in Books 1–3 includes:

Pre-Reading

Discussion
Vocabulary

Reading

Identifying Main Ideas and Details, Making Inferences
Reading Skill and Practice

Bridge Section—From Reading to Writing

Discussion, Vocabulary Review, Journal Writing

Writing

Writing Model or Examples
Writing Skills and Practice
Writing Assignment
Writing Process Steps

Book 4

Each unit of Book 4 includes:

Pre-Reading 1

Discussion
Vocabulary

Reading 1

Identifying Main Ideas and Details, Making Inferences
Reading and Vocabulary Skill and Practice

Bridge Section—From Reading to Writing

Discussion and Journal Writing

Pre-Reading 2

Discussion
Vocabulary

Reading 2

Identifying Main Ideas and Details, Making Inferences

Writing

Writing Model
Writing Skills and Practice
Writing Assignment
Writing Process Steps

Detailed Explanation of Parts, Books 1–3

Part 1, Reading

In the Pre-Reading section, students build schema by discussing the theme and studying key vocabulary before reading. High-interest readings and lively activities engage students as they develop vocabulary and reading skills and strategies that can be used in their own writing.

Bridge Section—From Reading to Writing

The Reflecting on the Reading activity focuses on content from the reading and how it can be applied to student writing. In some levels, a journal activity provides an opportunity for freewriting. Students use target vocabulary and explore a question from the reflection activity. Some levels also include exercises to activate vocabulary. Students are asked questions using target vocabulary and are encouraged to use their answers in the upcoming writing assignment.

Part 2, Writing

Writing models and writing skills practice allow students to hone their writing skills before they produce their own writing. In the writing assignment, students are led step-by-step through the writing process. This encourages them to gather ideas, focus and organize, and revise and edit their writing. This step-by-step process facilitates collaboration with classmates and the instructor and also promotes self-evaluation of writing.

Benefits to Students

This sequence of activities, common to Books 1–3, has at its core a set of essential competencies for pre-academic English learners that are emphasized throughout the four-book series. Upon completion of the activities, students will be prepared to:

- Recognize and produce a variety of sentences to express ideas (Books 1–2)

- Recognize and utilize the steps in the writing process to produce a composition (Books 2–4)

- Use ideas and language gained from reading in writing and speaking (Books 1–4)

- Organize and write a composition with a main idea and supporting ideas (Books 1–4)

- Recognize and use connectors and other devices that show relationships among ideas in texts (Books 1–4)

- Recognize and express the main idea and supporting details of a reading (Books 1–4)

Vocabulary Focus

The *From Reading to Writing* series also features a strong focus on vocabulary development. The high-frequency vocabulary targeted in each book is derived from three highly recognized vocabulary lists:
- West's *General Service List* (1953) of the 2,000 most frequently used words in English
- Coxhead's *Academic Word List* (2000) of the 570 most common word families
- Dilin Liu's list of most common idioms (2003)

Vocabulary experts agree that academic-bound students who acquire the words on the West and Coxhead lists will know more than 90 percent of the words they will encounter in academic texts (Nation, 2000). Furthermore, research studies have shown that repeated exposure to new words, and application of new vocabulary in writing and speech, increase the chances that students will acquire the target words (N. Schmitt, Nation, Laufer).

From Reading to Writing stresses vocabulary acquisition by providing opportunities for students to encounter, study, and use new words in each of these sections of a chapter or unit:
- Pre-Reading vocabulary activities
- Reading
- From Reading to Writing bridge section
- Post-Reading vocabulary review

Writing Resources

A full complement of appendices serve as resources for student writers. These include a section on Avoiding Plagiarism; a Grammar Reference; a Correction Symbols chart, which presents commonly used correction marks; a Vocabulary Review for each chapter; and an alphabetized Word List of target vocabulary. Additionally an online e-rater allows students to submit their compositions and receive prompt, individualized feedback.

References

Coxhead, A. (2000). "A New Academic Word List." *TESOL Quarterly*, 34(2), 213–38.

Laufer, B. (2003). "Vocabulary Acquisition in a Second Language: Do Learners Really Acquire Most Vocabulary by Reading?" *Canadian Modern Language Review* 59, 4: 565–585.

Liu, Dilin. (2003). "The Most Frequently Used Spoken American English Idioms: A Corpus Analysis and Its Implications." *TESOL Quarterly* 37, 671–700.

Mlynarcyzk, Rebecca. (1993). "Conversations of the Mind: A Study of the Reading/Writing Journals of Bilingual College Students." Diss. New York U, *DAI* 54, 4004A.

Nation, I. S. P. (2001). *Learning Vocabulary in Another Language.* Cambridge: Cambridge University Press.

Schmitt, N. (2000). *Vocabulary in Language Teaching.* Cambridge: Cambridge University Press.

Schmitt, N. & McCarthy, M. (Eds.). (1997). *Vocabulary: Description, Acquisition, and Pedagogy.* Cambridge: Cambridge University Press.

Spack, Ruth. (1993). "Student Meets Text, Text Meets Student: Finding a Way into Academic Discourse." *Reading in the Composition Classroom: Second Language Perspectives.* Joan G. Carson and Ilona Leki (Eds.). Boston: Heinle, 183–96.

Scope and Sequence

Unit		Reading	Reading Skills	Writing Skills	Writing Assignment
1	Health	Chapter 1 *Divided Sleep*	Skimming for Main Ideas	Organizing a unified paragraph	Write a descriptive paragraph about sleep habits
		Chapter 2 *Long Life*		Writing an effective topic sentence	Write a descriptive paragraph about a healthy/unhealthy lifestyle
2	Clothing	Chapter 3 *The Necktie*	Separating Fact from Opinion	Organizing an opinion paragraph	Write an opinion paragraph about clothing
		Chapter 4 *A Young Man and His Kilt*		Using connectors to express reasons	Write an opinion paragraph about dress codes
3	Great Minds	Chapter 5 *The Right-Brain, Left-Brain Controversy*	Scanning	Organizing an expository essay	Write an expository essay about a person's characteristics
		Chapter 6 *Artists as Scientists and Entrepreneurs*		Writing an effective thesis statement	Write an expository essay about the skills of an artist, a scientist, or a businessperson
4	Leisure	Chapter 7 *The Art of Paintball*	Recognizing Repetition of Ideas	Writing an introduction for a process essay	Write an introduction for a process essay about how to play a sport or game or do a leisure-time activity
		Chapter 8 *Camping in Oz*		Writing the body and conclusion of a process essay	Write a process essay about how to play a sport or game or do a leisure-time activity

Unit		Reading	Reading Skills	Writing Skills	Writing Assignment
5	Relationships	Chapter 9 *Six Degrees of Separation*	Recognizing Cohesive Devices	Summarizing	Write a summary
		Chapter 10 *Table for Two*		Writing a response to a reading	Write a personal response
6	Money Matters	Chapter 11 *Generation Broke*	Identifying Cause and Effect	Organizing a cause-effect essay Writing a proposal	Write a proposal and outline for a cause and effect essay about a financial situation or spending habits
		Chapter 12 *The IKEA Success Story*		Using hedge words	Write a cause and effect essay about a financial situation or spending habits
7	Generations	Chapter 13 *The Newest Generation at Work*	Distinguishing Generalizations from Support	Organizing a comparison-contrast essay	Write a proposal and outline for an essay to compare and contrast work situations or living situations
		Chapter 14 *Staying Home with Momma*		Using comparison and contrast expressions	Write an essay to compare and contrast work situations or living situations
8	Literature	Chapter 15 *Bliss (Part 1)*	Using Literary Terms	Writing a character analysis Using appositives	Write a character analysis paragraph
		Chapter 16 *Bliss (Part 2)*		Organizing a character analysis essay	Write a literary analysis essay about a character in a book, movie, or television show

UNIT ONE

Health

Divided Sleep

*In this chapter
you will:*

• read an essay
about sleep
patterns

• learn to skim a
reading for main
ideas

• organize and
write a unified
paragraph

A Woman Asleep *(1657) by Jan Vermeer*

PRE-READING

Discussion

Discuss the questions in pairs or small groups.

1. Look at the painting. Is this person having a good sleep? Explain your answer.
2. What are your usual sleep habits?
3. Why do you think people have trouble sleeping?

Vocabulary

Read the sentences. Match the boldfaced words with the definitions.

__*a*__ 1. College students are too busy to sleep much. Studying, working, and taking care of families **contribute to** their lack of sleep.

____ 2. Ari can **function** well on little sleep. He feels rested and awake after sleeping only three to four hours.

____ 3. Doctors **consider** exercise important for health and recommend exercising at least three times a week.

____ 4. Most people read indoors by **artificial** light, but I prefer to read outside under natural sunlight.

____ 5. If you're an "early bird" who likes to wake up early, it **makes sense** to take 8:00 A.M. classes instead of late-night classes.

____ 6. Mrs. Wood recently learned that she must **alter** her eating habits. She can no longer eat foods with high sugar content.

____ 7. **Researchers** have spent a great deal of time studying what happens to our bodies while we are sleeping.

____ 8. Does the **stress** of daily life keep you awake? Thinking about problems or responsibilities may make it hard to fall asleep.

---

  a. help to make something happen
  b. continuous feelings of worry that prevent you from relaxing
  c. not natural, but made by people
  d. have a clear meaning that is easy to understand
  e. have an opinion about something or someone
  f. people who study a subject in detail to discover new facts about it
  g. work in a particular way or in the correct way
  h. change in some way

**READING
SKILL**

Skimming for Main Ideas

Skimming is reading very quickly to identify the main ideas of an essay, article, or other reading. When readers skim, they try to understand only the most important ideas. They do not try to understand every detail.

Use these steps to skim a reading:
  • **Read the title.** The title of a reading often gives the main idea.
  • **Read the first paragraph.** An essay or article has an introduction—usually the first paragraph. Often, one sentence in the introduction gives the main idea.

- **Read the first sentences of the body, or middle, paragraphs.** The first sentence of each body paragraph usually gives the main idea of that paragraph.
- **Read the last paragraph.** Usually, the last paragraph is the conclusion. The conclusion usually includes one sentence that restates the main idea.

Practice

Skim the reading "Divided Sleep." Then answer the questions.

1. What is the main point of the reading? Circle the letter of the best answer.
   a. the amounts of sleep time
   b. the practice of divided sleep
   c. the problems of sleeping

2. Which paragraphs discuss these main ideas? Write the number of the paragraph next to each idea.
   __2__ a. what people did before they had electricity
   _____ b. the conclusion that divided sleep is a natural way to sleep
   _____ c. what one study tells us about divided sleep
   _____ d. what happened during *second sleep*
   _____ e. what happened between sleep periods

READING

Divided Sleep

1   People often complain about not getting "a good night's sleep," but sleep patterns differ from person to person. Most adults require six to eight hours of sleep to **function** well, while others survive on only a few hours. Still, most people today think of sleep as one continuous period of downtime.[1] This is not the way people used to sleep. According to **researchers**, in earlier times, people divided sleep by first sleeping a few hours, waking up, then going back to sleep.

2   Before the 18th century, people had no gas or electricity in their homes. Fire, candles, or oil lamps were the common forms of lighting. This lack of **artificial** lighting in homes **contributed to** people's sleep patterns. It **made sense** for people to go to bed early. If you lived in this time period, you might be a hard-working farmer, and you would come home, eat, and quickly fall into

....

[1] **downtime:** (slang) a period of rest or relaxation

bed exhausted. You would probably go to sleep at 9:00 or 10:00 P.M. In this first period of sleep—called *first sleep*—you would typically sleep until midnight or shortly afterwards.

3   Halfway through the night, you would wake up for an hour or more during a period some call the *watch*, or *watching period*. When you came out of first sleep, you would stay in bed and relax quietly. You might talk with a bedfellow, meditate[2] on the day's events or the meaning of a dream, or just let your mind wander.[3] If you enjoyed writing or drawing, you might get out of bed to write a poem or story or draw a picture.

4   Then you would start to feel sleepy, so you would return to bed and fall asleep again for your *second sleep*. This period would continue until early morning when daylight arrived. Again, with no artificial lighting in homes, people naturally woke up early to take advantage of sunlight.

5   Today, humans may **consider** divided sleep a strange habit, but sleep researchers say

that it is actually a more natural sleep pattern. Dr. Thomas Wehr of the U.S. National Institute of Mental Health has studied human sleep. He thinks that modern sleep problems occur because the older, natural way of sleeping is breaking through the more recent continuous sleep pattern. Wehr and other scientists believe that artificial lighting has **altered** the way people sleep. In a research study, he asked 15 adults to rest and sleep in darkness for 14 hours (from 6:00 P.M. to 8:00 A.M.) At first, the subjects took a few hours to get to sleep, and then slept 11 hours a night. Then, over time, they switched to divided sleep. They fell asleep for about three to five hours in the evening, stayed awake for an hour or two, and then slept again for four hours till early morning.

6   Unlike the people in the study, we modern humans generally do not practice divided sleep. However, many of us have the experience of waking up in the middle of the night. We usually consider this a sleeping "problem," but perhaps we should look at it as natural behavior. Divided sleep may be the way we should all be sleeping. A first sleep followed by a relaxation period and a second period of sleep could help all of us to beat the **stress** of our fast-paced lives.

---

[2]**meditate:** make yourself feel calm by being silent and still and thinking about one thing
[3]**let your mind wander:** no longer pay attention to one thing

Identifying Main Ideas

Read each question. Circle the letter of the best answer.

1. What is the main idea of the reading?
   a. People in the past did not sleep as well as people today.
   b. People in the past divided their sleep into two parts.
   c. People in the past woke up and relaxed during the night.
   d. People in the past fell asleep easily because of hard work.

2. What is the main purpose of paragraphs 2–4?
    a. to explain what happens in a night of divided sleep
    b. to give an opinion about the divided sleep pattern
    c. to describe the life of farmers before the 18th century
    d. to explain the lives of writers and artists before the 18th century

3. In paragraph 5, what does the research study suggest about divided sleep?
    a. Divided sleep is a strange way to sleep.
    b. Divided sleep occurs when people sleep with artificial lights.
    c. Divided sleep is a natural sleep pattern for humans.
    d. Divided sleep means sleeping 11 hours in one period.

4. What conclusion does the writer make about divided sleep?
    a. It is one type of sleeping problem.
    b. It may help people handle daily stress.
    c. It is not the best sleep pattern for everyone.
    d. It is a common practice in modern times.

Identifying Details

Each statement below is incorrect. Look at the reading again and correct each statement.

1. People had a divided sleep pattern ~~after~~ *before* the 18th century.

2. First sleep usually ended at about 9:00 P.M.

3. Before the 18th century, people had gas and electricity in their homes.

4. A researcher studied the sleep habits of 15 children.

5. Over time, the subjects in the study changed to continuous sleep.

Making Inferences

The following information is not directly stated in the reading. Infer what the writer would say is true. Check (✔) each statement the writer would agree with.

_____ 1. Most people today are familiar with the practice of divided sleep.

_____ 2. In the past, people thought of divided sleep as natural.

_____ 3. The watching period was enjoyable.

_____ 4. The modern practice of sleeping for one long period may explain why some people have sleep problems.

Reflecting on the Reading

Discuss the questions in pairs or small groups.

Journal
Choose one
question and
write a journal
entry.

1. The reading says that a continuous night of sleep is not a natural way to sleep. Do you believe that? Explain.
2. Have you or someone you know ever had a night of divided sleep? Describe the night of sleep.
3. Do you sometimes experience insomnia, or sleeplessness? Explain.

Activating Your Vocabulary

Take notes on these questions. Try to use your answers in your Writing Assignment.

Vocabulary
For more
practice with
vocabulary, go
to page 192.

1. What is your typical sleep pattern? Do you **consider** any part of that pattern a problem?
2. When you sleep well, what factors **contribute to** your rest? When you sleep poorly, what factors **contribute to** your sleep problems?
3. Would you like to **alter** your daily schedule in any way? If so, how?
4. Do you **function** well in the early morning? Why or why not?
5. What aspects of your life cause you **stress**?

WRITING

Read the model paragraph.

MODEL

My Sleep Problem

My greatest sleep problem is not falling asleep but staying asleep. At 10:00 or 11:00 P.M., I climb into bed with a book and a glass of water. I read for half an hour, which helps me to become drowsy. Then I drink some water, turn off the light, and have no trouble falling asleep. However, at 2:00 or 3:00 A.M.—like clockwork—I wake up with my mind alert, feeling wide awake. Sometimes, I lie in bed for two to three hours, trying to go back to sleep. Other times, I get out of bed and do some activity for one to two hours, like read or go on the Internet, thinking that I will get sleepy again and be able to return to sleep. However, I usually spend at least a half-hour lying awake in bed afterwards. When I wake up in the morning, I feel tired, like I've not had a good rest, and I feel groggy the whole day. I wish I could solve my problem and get a full night of sleep.

Organizing a Unified Paragraph

A paragraph has three important parts that make it **unified**, or focused on a particular subject: the topic sentence, the body, and the conclusion.

The **topic sentence** states the main idea or the most important thing that you want to say about the topic.

EXAMPLE

My greatest sleep problem is not falling asleep but staying asleep.

The **body** supports the main idea with sentences that explain the idea more fully. The body does not include sentences that do not support the topic sentence.

The **conclusion** ends the paragraph with a sentence that states the idea in the topic sentence in different words.

Practice

Read each paragraph and follow the steps. Then compare your answers in pairs.

1. Underline the topic sentence.
2. Mark the body of the paragraph in the margin. Include all the sentences that support the main idea.
3. Underline the conclusion.

Paragraph 1

Caffeine and Your Health

Coffee, colas, and caffeine drinks can affect your health negatively. For example, caffeine can have negative effects on your nutrition. Caffeinated beverages often replace more nutritious drinks like milk in your diet. In addition, coffee and other drinks with caffeine may also make you eat less. Caffeine contains an appetite suppressant. This chemical reduces your desire to eat. Small amounts of caffeine in your diet are acceptable. However, too much can harm your health.

Paragraph 2

Getting Relaxed

According to doctors, a simple two-step technique for relaxing the body may help you fall asleep more easily. They recommend a procedure that involves tightening and loosening muscle groups. You can do this in a sitting or a lying position. Begin by tightening the muscles in your right foot and keep them tight for a few seconds. Then loosen the muscles very slowly. Try to make these muscles feel as loose as possible. Do the same with the rest of your right leg. Gradually, add more muscle groups, moving from your feet and legs to your hands and arms, and then ending with your stomach, shoulders, and neck. Repeat the muscle-tightening and relaxing steps until you feel sleepy. This technique will help you to relax your body and fall asleep more quickly.

WRITING ASSIGNMENT

Write a paragraph. Follow the steps.

STEP 1   **Get ideas.**

A. Choose a topic for your paragraph. Check (✔) it.

❑ **Topic 1:**   Your typical sleep pattern

❑ **Topic 2:**   Your typical sleep problem

B. Follow the instructions for your topic.

Topic 1:   Circle the phrase below that best describes your *Typical Sleep Pattern*. Then complete the chart.

continuous sleep   **divided sleep**

Typical Sleep Pattern

TIME	ACTIVITY	DETAILS
	Go to bed	
	Fall asleep	
	Wake up	

Topic 2:   Make a chart like the one above to describe your *Typical Sleep Problem*. Include the *Time, Type of Problem,* and *Details* to describe the problem.

STEP 2   **Organize your ideas.**

A. Write a topic sentence that describes your typical sleep pattern or problem.

EXAMPLES

Topic 1:   On most nights, my sleep pattern is divided.

Topic 2:   I have trouble sleeping because my cat wants to join me in bed.

B. Choose ideas from Step 1 to support the topic sentence.

STEP 3   **Write a rough draft.**

Write your paragraph. Use the chart from Step 1. Include vocabulary from the chapter where possible.

STEP 4   **Revise your rough draft.**

Read your paragraph. Use the Writing Checklist to look for mistakes. Work alone or in pairs.

Writing Checklist

❑ Is your paragraph unified, or focused on one subject?

❑ Does your paragraph have a topic sentence?

❑ Does the body include sentences that support the main idea?

❑ Does your paragraph have a conclusion?

❑ Did you use correct paragraph format, such as adding a title and indenting the first line?

❑ Did you use vocabulary from the chapter appropriately?

STEP 5   **Edit your writing.**

A. Edit your paragraph. Correct any mistakes in capitalization, punctuation, spelling, or verb use.

B. Exchange paragraphs with a partner. Use the Correction Symbols on page 191 to mark each other's work.

EXAMPLE

VERB TENSE ERROR (v.t.)

have

Every night I usually ~~had~~ trouble falling asleep.

STEP 6   **Write a final copy.**

Correct your mistakes. Copy your final paragraph and give it to your instructor.

Long Life

*In this chapter
you will:*

• read an article
  about people
  who live long

• learn how to
  write an
  effective topic
  sentence

• write a unified
  paragraph

Elizabeth "Pampo" Israel of the Dominican Republic

PRE-READING

Discussion

Discuss the questions in pairs or small groups.

1. Look at the photograph. Elizabeth Israel died in 2003 at 128 years old. How do you think Israel lived in order to reach the age of 128?
2. Do you know a healthy elderly person? What does this person do to stay healthy?
3. In general, do you practice healthy or unhealthy habits? Explain.

Vocabulary

Read the boldfaced words and their definitions. Then complete the paragraph with the correct words or phrases.

a great deal:	a large quantity or amount of something
factor:	one of several things that influence or cause a situation
major:	very large or important when compared to similar things or people
overall:	generally; including everything
play a role in:	have an effect or influence on something
relatively:	to a particular degree when compared with something else
select:	choose something or someone
tend to:	be likely to do a particular thing

As a personal trainer in the college gymnasium, Joshua helps many people on campus to stay healthy. (1) _____*Overall*_____, his job is to help students and employees to use the gym correctly. However, he does much more than that. Joshua is studying physical education, so he has (2) _____ of knowledge about the human body. He uses his skill to help people (3) _____ the best exercises and equipment for their age and physical condition. He also teaches them to use the machinery. He (4) _____ start beginners out on the stationery bicycles because these are (5) _____ easy to use. Another (6) _____ part of his job is to lead exercise classes. Joshua is an important (7) _____ in the success of the gym operation because many students enroll in his hip-hop and salsa dance classes. Clearly, Joshua (8) _____ the health of many people at his college.

Long Life

1   More and more people are living to be centenarians, or 100 years old or older. Are they just lucky? Or are there **factors** that you can apply to your life? Recent research suggests that both young and old can learn **a great deal** from lifestyle habits that contribute to long life.

2   Worldwide, there has been a steady rise in centenarians. Since 1950, the number of 100-year-olds and over has doubled each decade.[1] In 2000, there were 167,000 centenarians, and by 2050 that number may reach 3.3 million. One million of these will be in Japan, and more than 450,000 will be in the United States. Those over the age of 100 will be the fastest growing age group.

Three Long-Living Groups

3   Researchers have tried to discover the secrets of a healthy long life. *National Geographic* journalist Dan Buettner traveled the world to find the "hot spots" of longevity.[2] He **selected** three groups of long-living people. These are the inhabitants of the mountain villages of Sardinia, the island of Okinawa, and the Seventh-Day Adventists[3] in California.

4   The long-living seniors in each place share key lifestyle habits. They don't smoke. They put family first. They **maintain** a social network of family and friends. They have daily physical activity, and they eat fruits, vegetables, and whole grains. Buettner found regional differences in practices[4] and beliefs, however.

Two Island Lifestyles

5   On Sardinia, an island in the Mediterranean Sea, more men live to be 100 plus than anywhere else in the world. Some scientists believe that a healthy, low-stress lifestyle explains their long lives. Most Sardinian males do physically hard farm work alongside their spouses. Typically, they drink red wine and eat cheese. Other experts say that the long life of Sardinians runs in families.[5]

6   On the Japanese island of Okinawa, there are four times as many centenarians as in the United States. The Okinawa Centenarian Study is studying more than 600 centenarians. Their low-calorie diet of miso,[6] whole-grain rice, vegetables, and soy appears to **play a role in** longevity. Okinawans also eat small amounts of food. In addition, researchers found that in Okinawa, centenarians live purposeful lives by working and living independently and keeping lifelong friends.

The Adventist Study

7   Dr. Gary Fraser directed the Adventist Health Study, following 34,000 Californian Seventh-Day Adventists for 12 years. On average, Adventist men lived 7.3 years longer than other Californians. Adventist women lived 4.4 years longer. Vegetarian Adventist men and women had even greater longevity,

(continued)

---

[1] **decade:** a period of time equal to ten years
[2] **longevity:** long life
[3] **Seventh Day Adventists:** a Christian religious group
[4] **practice:** something that people do often and in a particular way

---

[5] **runs in families:** If something such as a quality, disease, or skill runs in the family, many people in that family have it.
[6] **miso:** a thick paste made from soybeans

with up to 10 more years than the average Californian. Forty-eight percent of male vegetarians and 60 percent of female vegetarians in this group lived to age 85. **Overall**, in the United States, 20 percent of men and 39 percent of women live to age 85.

8   Fraser found that simple lifestyle behaviors contributed to long life. The seniors never smoked. They exercised regularly and maintained a healthy weight. They ate a vegetarian diet that included nuts and beans four times a week. One-hundred-year-olds were active and energetic. They enjoyed life, family relationships, and **relatively** good health.

9   What are their secrets? Is it their families, the food they eat, or their positive view of life? Perhaps it's all of these. There's also an advantage to having long-living parents. Siblings[7] and children of centenarians **tend to** live longer. But some research suggests long-living families may only be 30 to 40 percent of the equation.[8] The **major** factor is lifestyle. Your lifespan[9] depends on how you live. It's what and how much you eat, what you do, and how well you handle stress. You cannot change your families, but you can change to a more healthful lifestyle. During the next decade, we are likely to discover many more secrets of longevity. Some scientists believe that technology and research will help people live to the age of 125 and older. Meanwhile, following the behaviors of long-living people can add extra healthy years to your life.

----

[7] **sibling:** your brother or sister
[8] **equation:** the group of factors that causes longevity
[9] **lifespan:** the period between life and death

Identifying Main Ideas

Read each question. Circle the letter of the best answer.

1. What is the main idea of the reading?
   a. People live much longer in three specific areas of the world.
   b. People who live longer practice important lifestyle habits.
   c. People will live longer in the future because of technology.
   d. People with lifelong friends and close family ties live longer.

2. What is the writer's main purpose in paragraphs 3–6?
   a. to discover how diet may affect a person's lifespan
   b. to compare the habits of three groups of long-living people
   c. to identify the "hot spots" of longevity in the world
   d. to advise people to stop smoking and eating unhealthy foods

3. According to paragraph 8, what characterizes the behaviors of Adventists?
    a. They exercise regularly.
    b. They are in good health.
    c. They lead active lives.
    d. all of the above

4. In paragraph 9, what is the writer's conclusion about long life?
    a. People live longer mainly because of their families.
    b. People live longer mainly because of their lifestyles.
    c. People live longer mainly because of technology.
    d. People live longer mainly because of research.

Identifying Details

Check (✔) the groups that have these healthy habits.

Healthy Habits

	OKINAWANS	SARDINIANS	ADVENTISTS
don't smoke	✔	✔	✔
keep lifelong friends			
eat small amounts of food			
eat a lot of cheese			
eat plenty of vegetables			
keep physically active			

Making Inferences

The following information is not directly stated in the reading. Infer what the writer would say is true. Check (✔) each statement the writer would agree with.

_____ 1. Most people 100 or older are vegetarians.

_____ 2. Many older people need to change their lifestyles.

_____ 3. Overall, seniors eat unhealthy foods.

_____ 4. Centenarians lead low-stress lives.

_____ 5. Researchers who study longevity find out things that can help very few people.

Journal
Choose one
question and
write a journal
entry.

Reflecting on the Reading

Discuss the questions in pairs or small groups.

1. Which of the healthy activities in the chart on page 15 do you do? When, how often, and where do you practice these behaviors?
2. What are some ways that you could change your lifestyle to become healthier? Explain.
3. Do you think you will live to be 100 years old? Why or why not? Explain.

Vocabulary
For more
practice with
vocabulary, go
to page 193.

Activating Your Vocabulary

Take notes on these questions. Try to use your answers in your Writing Assignment.

1. **Overall**, do you practice healthy or unhealthy eating habits? Explain.
2. Do you **tend to** eat well or poorly? Explain.
3. Is stress a **major factor** in your life? Why or why not?
4. How can you get **a great deal** of exercise if you live in a city?
5. Do you think a person's family history **plays a role in** his or her health? In what ways?
6. If you are a **relatively** active person, does that affect your health in a positive or a negative way? Explain.

WRITING

WRITING SKILL

Writing an Effective Topic Sentence

The topic sentence of a paragraph states the main idea of the paragraph. It has two important parts: the **topic** (the general idea) and the **controlling idea** (what the writer will say about the topic).

EXAMPLE

┌ TOPIC ┐┌────────────── CONTROLLING IDEA ──────────────┐
My diet includes at least five servings of fruits and vegetables.

The topic is *my diet*. The controlling idea is *includes at least five servings of fruits and vegetables*. This second part of the statement controls the ideas that the writer includes in the paragraph.

The same topic can have a different controlling idea. The writer might begin with the topic sentence below. Then the supporting sentences and conclusion in the paragraph would be different.

EXAMPLE

┌ TOPIC ┐┌──────────────── CONTROLLING IDEA ────────────────┐
My diet includes a large breakfast and lunch and a light dinner.

Practice

A. Circle the topic and underline the controlling idea in each topic sentence.

1. The best types of exercise are walking and riding a bicycle.

2. Eating healthy foods is difficult for me.

3. Health-conscious people have several techniques for staying active.

4. Exercise gives me energy and helps me sleep well.

5. I play basketball regularly because it gives me two important benefits.

B. Circle the topic and underline the controlling idea in each topic sentence. Then add another supporting sentence that makes a different point.

1. Topic sentence: (Vegetarians) eat foods that are rich in vitamins and proteins.

   Supporting point 1: *Fruits are an important part of their diet.*

   Supporting point 2: *They also eat legumes in place of meat.*

   Supporting point 3: _____

   _____

2. Topic sentence: My energy level starts high, but it decreases during the day.

   Supporting point 1: *I wake up early with lots of energy.*

   Supporting point 2: *At midday, I eat lunch and drink coffee to maintain my energy.*

   Supporting point 3: _____

   _____

3. Topic sentence: I have trouble sleeping for several reasons.

Supporting point 1: *First, I live on a noisy street.*

Supporting point 2: *Another problem is my uncomfortable bed.*

Supporting point 3: _____

_____

C. *Write a topic sentence with a controlling idea for each paragraph.*

Paragraph 1

The Tiger Woods Workout

_____

_____

The first part of his workout is 30 minutes of cardiovascular exercise. This type of exercise warms his body up and keeps his heart strong. Woods usually does this by riding a stationary bicycle. Next, he does at least 30 minutes of total-body stretching. He needs to keep his arms, legs, and knees strong to play golf. By stretching, Woods maintains the strength in his backbone and knee joints. These two techniques have helped him to stay in good physical shape so that he can succeed in his career as a professional golfer.

Paragraph 2

Fast Food or *Fat* Food?

_____

_____

One way to make fast food healthier for you is to choose items with less fat. Avoid fried foods like fried-fish sandwiches with mayonnaise, fried chicken strips, or French fries and onion rings. Instead, select a grilled fish sandwich and leave off the cheese, bacon, sauce, or mayonnaise. Another option is to order a salad with fresh vegetables or grilled chicken. It's also a good idea to limit the sugary foods on fast-food menus. Stay away from the desserts and milkshakes, and drink water instead of soft drinks. Use less ketchup on sandwiches, and skip the honey on chicken. If you follow these tips, your fast food won't turn into *fat* food.

Write a paragraph. Follow the steps.

STEP 1 **Get ideas.**

A. Choose a topic for your paragraph. Check (✔) it.

☐ **Topic 1:** Two ways to live longer

☐ **Topic 2:** Two unhealthy habits

B. Complete the chart on your topic.

Topic Title

_____

TYPE OF ACTIVITY	SUPPORT

STEP 2 **Organize your ideas.**

A. Write a topic sentence that states your topic and the controlling idea.

EXAMPLES

Topic 1: Running and eating low-fat foods are two good ways for people to live longer.

Topic 2: Eating junk food and smoking are bad for people's health.

B. Choose ideas from Step 1 to support the topic sentence.

STEP 3 **Write a rough draft.**

Write your paragraph. Use the chart from Step 1. Include vocabulary from the chapter where possible.

STEP 4 Revise your rough draft.

Read your paragraph. Use the Writing Checklist to look for mistakes. Work alone or in pairs.

Writing Checklist

❑ Does your paragraph have a topic sentence that states the topic and controlling idea?

❑ Did you include supporting sentences to tell more about your topic sentence?

❑ Did you add a conclusion?

❑ Is your paragraph unified, or focused on one subject?

❑ Did you use vocabulary from the chapter appropriately?

STEP 5 Edit your writing.

A. Edit your paragraph. Correct any mistakes in capitalization, punctuation, spelling, or verb use.

B. Exchange paragraphs with a partner. Use the Correction Symbols on page 191 to mark each other's work.

EXAMPLE

VERB TENSE ERROR (v.t.)

smoked

My grandfather ~~smoke~~ cigarettes, and he died when he was young.

STEP 6 Write a final copy.

Correct your mistakes. Copy your final paragraph and give it to your instructor.

UNIT TWO

Clothing

The Necktie

PRE-READING

Discussion

Discuss the questions in pairs or small groups.

1. Look at the photograph. What do you think this man does for a living?
2. Why do you think men wear neckties?
3. What items of clothing do you especially like or dislike? Explain.

Vocabulary

Read the sentences. Match the boldfaced words with the definitions.

__d__ 1. Tran used to live in a warm climate. She lives in a cold region now, so she has **adopted** a different way of dressing.

_____ 2. When I travel, comfortable walking shoes are my most **essential** piece of clothing. I take them with me on all my trips.

_____ 3. People around the world use umbrellas to protect themselves from rain or sun. It's a **universal** custom.

_____ 4. Jin was wearing his heaviest coat on a snowy, windy day. **Nevertheless**, he felt cold.

_____ 5. That woman is wearing new, high-heeled shoes. **Consequently**, she is having trouble walking up the stairs.

_____ 6. Many people like to wear designer-label clothing. They want to show that they have money and high **status** in the society.

_____ 7. In many countries, a woman wears a ring on her left hand to **symbolize** that she is married.

_____ 8. **Due to** the heat, I wore light-colored clothing to the picnic. Dark-colored clothing makes me feel hot.

_____ 9. In her new office job, Nadiq feels a lot of **pressure** to wear nice clothes. Her company requires all workers to dress professionally.

_____ 10. Many people would like to **get rid of** their gray hair.

---

a. as a result
b. represent, stand for
c. because of
d. begin to use a new way of doing something
e. relating to everywhere in the world
f. a social position that makes people recognize and respect you
g. the use of strong words or arguments to try to get someone to do something
h. important and necessary
i. make something unwanted go away
j. in spite of that

The Necktie

1   Is there any item of apparel[1] more useless than a necktie? Why do intelligent men loop rags[2] around their necks and tighten them? U.S. journalist Linda Ellerbee asked, "If men can run the world, why can't they stop wearing neckties?" The answer is that men, like women, do many silly[3] things in the name of fashion. The necktie may be useless, but it remains popular because of **pressures** of fashion and social **status**.

2   There can be no argument that today's necktie is useless. A tie does not protect the body from the heat or cold, as a hat, shirt, pants, and shoes do. A tie is a thin strip of cloth, so it is not large enough to cover the body from bad weather. Also, it does not hold up other clothing items, like a belt does. A tie hangs from the top of a shirt, so it holds nothing up. A tie does not provide any comfort to the wearer, unlike socks, which allow a person to wear shoes comfortably. In fact, most men say that neckties are uncomfortable. Clearly, the tie has no practical purpose.

3   The tie hasn't always been useless, however. At one time, people wore neck coverings for a reason. Ties protected them from nature and even attack. In second-century Rome, speakers and soldiers wore neck scarves called *fascalias* to cover their throats from heat, cold, and dust. Later, Croatians[4] **adopted** the Roman neck cloths to guard against the weather. In 18th-century[5] England, neck cloths were so thick that they reportedly prevented injuries in battle. From Asia to North and South America, bandanas[6] have served as practical means of protecting working men's necks.

4   As time passed, though, the tie lost its usefulness. In the 1600s, men wore ties only because they **symbolized** the fashion of the upper class. King Louis XIV of France[7] wore lace and fine silk neck coverings. **Consequently**, many men followed the king's style. European paintings of the 17th to 19th centuries show men belonging to the military, government, and upper class in neck cloths so high and stiff that they could barely turn their heads. However, in the end, neck cloths became **essential** clothing for well-dressed men.

5   Many men today also wear neckties as a result of their desire for upward status in certain professions. Hopeful executives, clerks, and technicians wear neckties because their *bosses* do. These men wear ties to show their membership in business, politics, and other professions. Why does tradition force these men to hang this scrap of fabric around their necks? Many men do it to achieve success or attract attention from their bosses.

6   **Due to** these pressures, the tyranny[8] of the tie has spread across the globe. A necktie

---

[1] **apparel:** clothing
[2] **rags:** small pieces of old cloth
[3] **silly:** not sensible or serious
[4] **Croatians:** people of Croatia, an Eastern European country

[5] **18th century:** the years 1700 to 1799
[6] **bandana:** a neck scarf, usually made of cotton
[7] **King Louis XIV (the 14th):** the ruler of France 1643–1715
[8] **tyranny:** strict, unfair, and often cruel control over someone

is a necessary part of formal male attire[9] in Asia, Africa, and South America. In fact, people in China and Japan now think a man without a tie is not serious about work and believe that he disrespects tradition. Their parents and grandparents had never even heard of the tie. In nearly every corner of the world, the many varieties of neck coverings have disappeared. Now there is one **universal** shape and style that dominates the world of neckwear.

7   Despite these pressures, some people have tried to **get rid of** ties. Many companies allow their workers to dress more casually on Fridays, so that is a day when male professionals may go to work without ties. Also, men sometimes dress in shirts without ties in the summer when it is hot. And in more and more workplaces today, men are no longer expected to wear ties at all.

8   **Nevertheless**, many men are still expected to wear ties to work. They look in the mirror, fix their necktie, and tighten it like a noose.[10] Centuries, or perhaps just decades from today, people will look back and shake their heads in disbelief. They will not be able to understand why men actually put these things around their necks and thought them necessary to wear. So why are men in today's world considered inappropriately[11] dressed if they appear at a business meeting or a wedding without a tie? Perhaps those men care more about their own comfort than about fashion and don't want to follow the rules. After all, it's the 21st century!

---

[10] **noose:** a circle of rope that becomes tighter as it is pulled, used for hanging people as a punishment
[11] **inappropriately:** not right for a particular situation or person

---

[9] **attire:** clothing

Identifying Main Ideas

Read each question. Circle the letter of the best answer.

1. What is the main idea of the reading?
   a. The necktie was very popular among upper-class men.
   b. The necktie is worn by men around the world.
   c. The necktie once protected men from nature.
   d. The necktie is useless but still remains popular.

2. What is the main idea in paragraph 2?
   a. Neckties have no purpose.
   b. Ties do not hold up other pieces of clothing.
   c. Ties do not protect the body.
   d. Ties are not comfortable.

3. What is the main idea in paragraph 3?
   a. Neckties used to serve a purpose.
   b. Neckties prevented injuries in battle.
   c. Neckties were used all over the world.
   d. Neckties were called *fascalias* in ancient Rome.

4. According to paragraph 8, what will happen to neckties in the future?
   a. People will continue to wear them.
   b. People will understand their purpose.
   c. People will criticize men who wear ties.
   d. People will wonder why they were popular.

5. What is the best description of the reading?
   a. a report that gives facts about the necktie
   b. a description of types of neckties
   c. an essay that criticizes the use of neckties
   d. an explanation about the use of neckties

Identifying Details

Mark the statements T (True) or F (False). Correct the false statements.

_____ 1. Roman neck coverings protected their wearers.

_____ 2. Fancy neck coverings did not exist in Europe in the 1800s.

_____ 3. In 17th century Europe, military men wore neck coverings.

_____ 4. Neckties are a traditional item of apparel in Japan.

_____ 5. In the summer, men may wear shirts without ties to work.

Making Inferences

The following information is not directly stated in the reading. Infer what the writer would say is true. Check (✔) each statement the writer would agree with.

_____ 1. Most men do not really want to wear neckties.

_____ 2. King Louis XIV of France had practical reasons for wearing a tie.

_____ 3. Men wear neckties to show that they are different.

_____ 4. Neckties have existed in Africa and Asia for a long time.

_____ 5. In the future, men may stop wearing ties.

READING SKILL

Separating Fact from Opinion

"The Necktie" presents facts and opinions about neckties. This chart gives examples of both facts and opinions from the reading.

EXAMPLES

Facts	Opinions
In the 1600s, King Louis XIV wore a necktie.	Wearing a necktie makes a man look like a king.
A necktie is a thin piece of cloth worn around the neck.	A necktie is an uncomfortable rag worn around the neck.
Men all over the world wear neckties.	Men should not wear neckties.

A **fact** is something that is known to be true. Statements of fact:
- often tell about past or present events.
- can be checked in a source or by observation.

An **opinion** expresses a person's belief. Opinion statements:
- include an idea that people can agree or disagree with. The idea may be expressed through adjectives such as *useless* or *uncomfortable*.
- often include the modal verbs *may, might, could, should,* or *must. May, might,* and *could* express the writer's belief that something will possibly happen. *Should* and *must* express a writer's recommendation or call to action.

Practice

A. Mark the statements F (Fact) or O (Opinion). Reread the paragraphs in "The Necktie" if necessary.

_____ 1. Is there any item of apparel more useless than a necktie? (paragraph 1)

_____ 2. Men, like women, do many silly things in the name of fashion. (paragraph 1)

_____ 3. The tie hangs from the top of a shirt, holding nothing up. (paragraph 2)

_____ 4. In second-century Rome, speakers and soldiers wore neck scarves. (paragraph 3)

_____ 5. European paintings of the 17th to 19th centuries show men belonging to the military, government, and upper class in neck cloths. (paragraph 4)

B. Work in pairs. Check your answers.

Reflecting on the Reading

Discuss the questions in pairs or small groups.

Journal
Choose one
question and
write a journal
entry.

1. The reading says that men who do not wear ties to business meetings are "considered inappropriately dressed." Do you agree? Explain.
2. Some companies encourage businessmen not to wear suits and ties in hot weather. Is that a good idea? Explain.
3. Do you believe that ties will continue to be popular? Why or why not?

Activating Your Vocabulary

Take notes on these questions. Try to use your answers in your Writing Assignment.

Vocabulary
For more
practice with
vocabulary, go
to page 194.

1. What is the most **essential** item of clothing that you own?
2. Think of one **universal** piece of clothing that all people you know wear. What is this item?
3. Which things that people buy show their social **status**?
4. What is one item of clothing that **symbolizes** the traditions of a culture that you know?
5. Have you **adopted** any bad habit in the clothes you wear or buy?

WRITING

Read the model paragraph.

MODEL

The Galabia

The *galabia* robe, a long cotton robe worn by men and women, is perfectly suited to both the culture and the climate of Egypt. Many traditional Muslims cover their bodies, so the long, flowing robes are absolutely ideal. They are long enough to cover the arms and legs, and many men and women also wear head coverings with them. Also, the fabric and style of the galabias make them appropriate for a hot

climate. The robes are made of lightweight cloth and come in many colors, especially white and light colors that are designed to repel the scorching hot sun. The loose fit of the galabia allows for free movement of the body, another way of keeping women and men cool even in the summer months. Clearly, the galabia suits the culture and climate of Egypt, making it perfect attire for the people who live there.

Organizing an Opinion Paragraph

WRITING SKILL

An **opinion** paragraph presents a writer's opinions about a situation or an event. It should have a topic sentence with a controlling idea, supported by reasons.

The topic sentence expresses your opinion about the topic in the controlling idea.

EXAMPLE

┌──── TOPIC ────┐

The *galabia* robe, a long cotton robe worn by men and women,

┌──────── CONTROLLING IDEA (OPINION) ────────┐

is perfectly suited to both the culture and the climate of Egypt.

Support your opinion with reasons and with sentences to explain your reasons. Reasons can be facts or opinions, but your paragraph will be stronger if it has more facts. Include explanations to give more information about your reasons.

EXAMPLES

The *galabia* robe is perfectly suited to both the culture and climate of Egypt. (topic sentence)

┌──── FACT ────┐ ┌──── OPINION ────┐

Muslims cover their bodies, so the long, flowing *galabias* are ideal. (reason)

┌──────── FACT ────────┐

They are long enough to cover the arms and legs, and many men and women also wear head coverings with them. (explanation)

End your paragraph with a concluding sentence that restates your opinion. This opinion is the main point of your writing, so you emphasize it by restating it.

EXAMPLE

┌──────── CONCLUDING SENTENCE ────────┐

Clearly, the *galabia* suits the culture and climate of Egypt, making it perfect attire for the people who live there.

Practice

A. *Read the model paragraph on pages 28–29 again. Circle the words in the topic sentence that express the writer's opinion. Underline the writer's second reason for this opinion and the sentences to explain that reason.*

B. *Underline the controlling ideas in these topic sentences. Then cross out any sentences that do not support the topic sentence. Compare your answers with a partner's.*

1. Hats or caps <u>are not appropriate apparel for classrooms</u>.
   a. Wearing a hat or a cap in a classroom is disrespectful.
   b. ~~A hat or a cap can also keep a person's head warm when it's cold~~.
   c. Wearing a hat or cap is also unnecessary inside a building.

2. Blue jeans are very popular, but they are the world's most uncomfortable piece of clothing.
   a. The blue jean fabric is hard and stiff, so you can't move easily.
   b. Some blue jeans are tight, so they are uncomfortable.
   c. Blue jeans are thick, so they keep you warm in the winter.

3. Online stores are great for books, but they are not the best places to buy clothes.
   a. Often, clothes don't look the same in photographs as they do in real life.
   b. Buying clothes on the Internet is easier than buying them in a store.
   c. It's important to try on clothes in person to make sure that they fit.

4. Some of my friends need to stop buying so many clothes.
   a. They always have stylish, new outfits.
   b. They have no more room in their closets.
   c. They are spending too much money.

C. *Work in pairs. Choose a topic sentence from Exercise B. Discuss supporting reasons and write one or two sentences of explanation to support each reason.*

Topic sentence: *Hats or caps are not appropriate apparel for classrooms.*

Reason: *Wearing a hat or a cap in a classroom is disrespectful.*

Explanation: *A hat may block the view of other classmates. They may not be able to see the instructor or the board.*

Write a paragraph. Follow the steps.

STEP 1   **Get ideas.**

A. Choose a topic for your paragraph. Check (✔) it.

❑ **Topic 1:**   An opinion about an item of clothing

❑ **Topic 2:**   An opinion about buying clothes

B. Write your opinions about your topic. Then choose one opinion to use in your paragraph. List reasons to support that opinion.

EXAMPLES

Topic 1:	Opinion:	Students should not wear shorts to class.
	Reasons:	Shorts look too informal.
		They can distract the teacher.
Topic 2:	Opinion:	Large department stores are the best places to buy clothing.
	Reasons:	There are a lot of different types of clothing.
		The different clothing is all in one store, so it saves time.

STEP 2   **Organize your ideas.**

A. Write your opinion in a topic sentence with a controlling idea.

B. Choose two reasons from your list in Step 1 to support your opinion.

C. Think of more ideas to explain each reason.

STEP 3   **Write a rough draft.**

Write your paragraph. Use your sentences from Step 2 to help you. Include vocabulary from the chapter where possible.

STEP 4 Revise your rough draft.

Read your paragraph. Use the Writing Checklist to look for mistakes. Work alone or in pairs.

Writing Checklist

❑ Does your paragraph have a topic sentence, supporting ideas, and a concluding sentence?

❑ Does your topic sentence give an opinion?

❑ Did you include reasons to support your opinion?

❑ Did you add sentences to explain each reason?

❑ Did you use correct paragraph format, such as adding a title and indenting the first line?

❑ Did you use vocabulary from the chapter appropriately?

STEP 5 Edit your writing.

A. Edit your paragraph. Correct any mistakes in capitalization, punctuation, spelling, or verb use.

B. Exchange paragraphs with a partner. Use the Correction Symbols on page 191 to mark each other's work.

EXAMPLE

SPELLING ERROR (sp.)

breathe

Sometimes my blue jeans feel very tight. I can't ~~breath~~.

STEP 6 Write a final copy.

Correct your mistakes. Copy your final paragraph and give it to your instructor.

A Young Man and His Kilt

A Scottish kilt

PRE-READING

Discussion

Discuss the questions in pairs or small groups.

1. Look at the photograph. What do you know about kilts?
2. Is the young man's kilt appropriate for a high school dance? Explain.
3. Many schools have rules about clothing. Do you think schools should allow students to wear whatever clothes they like? Explain.

Vocabulary

Read these paragraphs. Write the boldfaced words next to the definitions below.

1. Some people like to **express** themselves by wearing different clothing. At a **formal** event like a graduation, the important thing is to choose clothing that is **appropriate** for the **occasion**. If you wear inappropriate clothing, someone is certain to make a negative **comment**.

2. Work or school clothing rules often cause **debate** about freedom, symbols, and cultural dress. A company or a school has the **authority** to tell workers or students how to dress. Students often try to change their school's **dress code**, however, so that they can wear what they like.

3. In Scotland, men wear kilts to show their national **pride**. In the past, however, the English rulers made it illegal to wear kilts. The Scots **struggled** to change the law, and now they wear kilts whenever they like.

a. _____ = discussion of a subject that often continues for a long time and in which people express different opinions

b. _____ = a standard of what you should wear for a particular situation

c. _____ = try very hard to achieve something even though it is difficult

d. _____ = correct or good for a particular time, situation, or purpose

e. ___*express*___ = use words or actions to show feelings or emotions

f. _____ = a stated opinion about something or someone

g. _____ = power someone has because of his or her official position

h. _____ = feeling that you like and respect yourself and deserve others' respect

i. _____ = used for official events or serious situations

j. _____ = an important event or ceremony

A Young Man and His Kilt

1   JACKSON, MISSOURI—Nathan Warmack wanted to honor his family history, so he decided to wear a Scottish kilt to his high school dance. Then a principal told him to change into a pair of pants.

2   The young man's case has resulted in an international **debate** about freedom, symbols, and cultural dress. More than 1,600 people have signed an Internet petition.[1] They want the school to apologize to the young man for not letting him wear the kilt to his senior prom.[2] Also, the young man's family is trying to change the school's **dress code** policy.

3   "It's a kilt. It's going to turn heads,[3] but I never believed it would have become what it is," Warmack said.

4   Other schools around the country also have **struggled** with the issue. A principal in Victoria, Texas, ordered two boys into "more **appropriate**" attire when they wore kilts to school in 1992.

5   In 1993, a student in Fayette County, Georgia, could not enter his prom at McIntosh High School because he showed up in a kilt and refused to change clothes.

6   A superintendent at Franklin Community High School in Indiana allowed a few boys to wear skirts to class in 1997. The superintendent said different people **express** themselves in different ways.

7   Warmack, a football player, lives in Jackson, Missouri. It's a growing, largely middle-class city of about 14,000 people about 100 miles from St. Louis. He got interested in his Scottish family after he saw Mel Gibson's 1995 movie *Braveheart*. The movie is about a Scottish battle to overthrow English rule. Warmack reads books about Scotland and visits websites to learn more about his family history.

8   He bought a kilt on the Internet to wear to his school's **formal** "Silver Arrow" dance in November. Warmack said he showed it to a vice principal before the dance. The vice principal joked that he should wear something underneath it. Warmack told him he would.

9   Warmack's parents, Terry and Paula, helped him piece together the rest of his outfit. It included a white shirt and black tie with white socks and black boots.

10   "We wanted it to be acceptable for the occasion," his father said.

11   Before the day of the dance, Nathan Warmack and his date posed for pictures. Then principal Rick McClard told the student he had to go change. McClard had not seen the kilt before. Warmack refused a few times and said the outfit recognized his family history.

12   Warmack claims McClard told him, "Well, this is my dance, and I'm not going to have students coming into it looking like

[1] **petition:** a piece of paper that asks someone in authority to do or change something and is signed by a lot of people

[2] **prom:** a formal dance party for high school students that usually happens at the end of a school year

[3] **to turn heads:** idiom—to cause people to stop what they are doing and turn their attention to something else

(continued)

clowns." According to Warmack's dad, McClard later said he had no memory of saying that. The principal did not return phone calls seeking his **comment**.

13   The school district's superintendent, Ron Anderson, said McClard has the **authority** to judge appropriate dress for after-school activities, including dances. That is because of the district's dress code policy.

14   "It's mainly to protect from the possibility of a disruption,"[4] Anderson said.

15   Several Scottish organizations are angry. They say the kilt is a symbol of Scottish **pride** and considered formal dress.

16   "To say the traditional Scottish dress makes you look like a clown is a direct insult to people of Scottish heritage[5] and those who live in Scotland," said Tom Wilson. He is a Texas commissioner for the Clan Gunn Society of North America, a Scottish organization.

---

[4] **disruption:** an unwelcome interruption

[5] **heritage:** the ideas, history, art, etc. of the people in a country or group that they pass to their children

Identifying Main Ideas

Read each question. Circle the letter of the best answer.

1. What is the main event that is reported in the reading?
   a. A young man decided to study his Scottish heritage.
   b. A young man wanted to wear a kilt to a school dance.
   c. A young man bought a Scottish kilt on the Internet.
   d. A young man asked someone to take pictures of him wearing a kilt.

2. In paragraph 2, what is the main point that the writer makes about the boy's kilt?
   a. It has led to an apology from a school.
   b. It is not acceptable clothing for a high school prom.
   c. It has caused changes to the dress code policy.
   d. It has resulted in a worldwide debate.

3. According to the superintendent, what was the main reason that school officials did not allow the young man to wear his kilt?
   a. The kilt represented Scottish heritage.
   b. The kilt might disrupt the school dance.
   c. The principal had not seen the kilt before.
   d. The kilt made the boy look like a clown.

Identifying Details

Mark the statements **T** *(True) or* **F** *(False). Correct the false statements.*

_____ 1. Nathan Warmack wanted to wear a kilt to his high school graduation.

_____ 2. More than 1,600 people signed a petition after the event.

_____ 3. A Texas school did not permit two boys to wear kilts to school.

_____ 4. The young man bought his kilt at a store.

_____ 5. The young man wore his kilt with a white shirt and white tie.

Making Inferences

The answers to the questions are not directly stated in the reading. Infer what the writer would say is true. Circle the letter of the best answer.

1. Why did so many people sign an Internet petition to support Nathan Warmack wearing a kilt?

   a. to show their support for teenagers

   b. to show their support of freedom of expression

2. What was the main reason that Nathan's parents supported his wearing a kilt?

   a. to show their support for their son

   b. to show their support of freedom of expression

3. Why is it often difficult for school officials to decide about dress rules?

   a. School officials think that most students dress appropriately.

   b. School officials want to balance student freedoms and rules.

4. Why didn't the school principal want to talk to news reporters?

   a. He did not want to discuss this controversial issue.

   b. He was unsure about his opinion on this issue.

Reflecting on the Reading

Read the summary of the school's dress code policy. Then discuss the questions in pairs or small groups.

School policy: School Superintendent Ron Anderson said that the principal can decide what students wear. The principal has the authority to tell students to change their clothing. This policy is the same for the classroom, a school dance, or any school activity.

1. Do you think the policy is fair? Explain.
2. The school superintendent said the dress code protects the school from "the possibility of a disruption." Do you think this is a good reason? Why or why not?
3. Where would wearing a kilt or other national dress be appropriate? Explain.

Activating Your Vocabulary

Take notes on these questions. Try to use your answers in your Writing Assignment.

1. What do you consider **appropriate** clothing for class?
2. Do you **express** yourself through the clothes that you wear? If so, in what ways?
3. Should parents have **authority** over their children's clothing? Explain.
4. What might people from your culture wear to show their cultural **pride**?

WRITING

**WRITING
SKILL**

Using Connectors to Express Reasons

Writers use **connectors** to link a situation, an event, or an opinion with the **reason** for it. These connecting words may come at the beginning or in the middle of sentences.

- ***Because*** **and** *since* **are followed by a subject + verb.** *Because* is usually used in the middle of a sentence to connect two sentences. *Since* usually comes at the beginning of a sentence.

SUBJECT ┌── VERB ──┐

I prefer wearing school uniforms **because** I don't waste time choosing what to wear.

SUBJECT   VERB

Since fashions change quickly, schools revise their dress codes often.

- *Because of* **is followed by a noun, noun phrase, or pronoun.** It can go at the beginning or the middle of the sentence.

EXAMPLES

┌────── NOUN PHRASE ──────┐

Because of the advantage of saving money on new school clothes, many parents support school-uniform policies.

Many parents support school-uniform policies **because of**

┌────── NOUN PHRASE ──────┐

the advantage of saving money on new school clothes.

- *So* **often connects two simple sentences.** A comma comes before the word *so* when it is used this way.

EXAMPLE

┌── SIMPLE SENTENCE ──┐   ┌── SIMPLE SENTENCE ──┐

School uniforms are expensive, **so** I do not think they should be required.

- *Therefore* **and** *as a result* **also connect two sentences.** They come after a period or a semi-colon and are followed by a comma.

EXAMPLES

We have to wear company T-shirts to work. **Therefore,** we don't need to buy extra work clothes.

My company makes all employees wear black pants; **as a result,** the workers must spend extra money on pants.

Practice

Complete each sentence with a connector that introduces the reason. Add commas where needed.

1. Students should not be allowed to wear shorts in school
   _____ shorts are not proper clothing for the classroom.
2. The store requires its workers to wear red shirts. _____
   it's easy for customers to find someone to help them.

3. _____ professors are examples to their students, they should dress in formal clothing.

4. People should buy winter coats in the spring instead of winter _____ the cheaper prices.

5. Sara hates shopping in stores, _____ she prefers to buy her clothes online.

WRITING ASSIGNMENT

Write a paragraph. Follow the steps.

STEP 1   **Get ideas.**

A. Choose a topic for your paragraph. Check (✔) it. Then list reasons for your opinion.

❑ **Topic 1:** Having or *not* having a dress code in a school or work setting.

❑ **Topic 2:** Allowing students or employees to have a say in creating a dress code for school or work.

B. Make a chart like the one below.

Types of Schools/ Workplaces	Typical Required Clothing	Topic 1: Is a dress code necessary?	Topic 2: Should people have a say?
cooking schools	hats		
factories	safety glasses		

C. Work in pairs. Compare your charts.

STEP 2   **Organize your ideas.**

A. Write a topic sentence for your paragraph that expresses your opinion.

EXAMPLE

Topic 1: Stores should require employees to wear shirts with the company name.

Topic 2: Students in high school should have a say in creating the school dress code.

B. Write reasons to support your opinion. Add one or two sentences of explanation to support each reason.

STEP 3   **Write a rough draft.**

Write your paragraph. Use your information from Step 2. Include vocabulary from the chapter where possible.

STEP 4   **Revise your rough draft.**

Read your paragraph. Use the Writing Checklist to look for mistakes. Work alone or in pairs.

Writing Checklist

❑ Does your paragraph have a topic sentence, supporting ideas, and a concluding sentence?

❑ Did you write a topic sentence that presents an opinion?

❑ Did you include reasons to support your opinion?

❑ Did you add sentences to explain each reason?

❑ Did you use connecting words that introduce reasons correctly?

❑ Did you use correct paragraph format, such as adding a title and indenting the first line?

❑ Did you use vocabulary from the chapter appropriately?

STEP 5   **Edit your writing.**

A. Edit your paragraph. Correct any mistakes in capitalization, punctuation, spelling, or verb use.

B. Exchange paragraphs with a partner. Use the Correction Symbols on page 191 to mark each other's work.

EXAMPLE

SPELLING ERROR (**sp.**)

strict

The school has a ~~strick~~ dress code. It requires students to wear uniforms.

STEP 6   **Write a final copy.**

Correct your mistakes. Copy your final paragraph and give it to your instructor.

UNIT THREE

Great Minds

The Right-Brain, Left-Brain Controversy

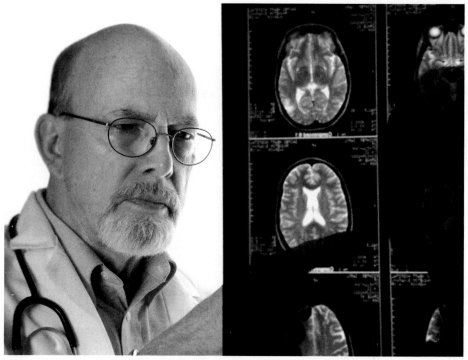

A scientist studies CAT scans of the brain.

PRE-READING

Discussion

Discuss the questions in pairs or small groups.

1. What is the doctor in the photograph looking at? What might scientists learn by studying X-ray photographs of the brain?

2. This chapter is titled "The Right-Brain, Left-Brain Controversy." What do you think this controversy might be about?

3. Which of these words or phrases best describe you: *logical, problem solver, creative, artistic, well-organized.* Explain your choice(s).

Vocabulary

Read the sentences. Match the boldfaced words with the definitions.

d 1. The use of lasers, or powerful lights, may soon **dominate** medicine and surgery.

____ 2. In the past few **decades**, computers have improved greatly. They are now smaller, faster, and cheaper.

____ 3. Science has **revealed** a great deal about how the brain works.

____ 4. Early scientists thought that the center of a person's intelligence was the heart rather than the brain, but later, scientists learned **otherwise**.

____ 5. Art can improve the lives of young people by helping them to become more **creative**.

____ 6. By increasing your mental **flexibility**, you become a more skilled thinker and problem solver.

____ 7. Many teenagers **display** physical problems like headaches or stomachaches when they get angry with their parents.

____ 8. Doing mathematical problems requires **logical** thought. You must think about the problems before you can solve them.

____ 9. Studies **indicate** that several parts of the brain work together to help us remember things.

____ 10. In psychology, information **processing** refers to the way we handle information.

---

a. make something known that was previously unknown
b. that the situation was different
c. reasonable and sensible
d. have the most influence or control
e. the method by which data is stored and organized
f. show that something is likely to be true
g. a period of time equal to 10 years
h. good at thinking of new ideas or making new things
i. ability to change or be changed easily to suit any new situation
j. let a feeling or quality be clearly seen

The Right-Brain, Left-Brain Controversy

1   Scientific study has shown that the brain has two sides. But does it also follow that, in each person, one side of the brain **dominates** the other and therefore causes each person's behavior? After the many **decades** of research, many scientists have begun to think **otherwise**. Now that these scientists know more about the brain, many now believe that the popular theories about "right-brain, left-brain" dominated behavior are most likely untrue.

2   Until recently, the idea of right brain- or left brain-dominated characteristics was a common belief among many scientists, too. The idea went something like this: A person with a dominant right brain was generally seen as **creative**, intuitive,[1] and artistic, a person who valued **flexibility** over stability.[2] In contrast, a person whose left brain was dominant was seen to be a **logical** problem-solver, someone who used reason rather than emotions to solve problems, and who excelled at using and learning language or mathematics. Right-brain and left-brain dominance was used to explain why we act the way we do.

3   Take a look at the "right-brain, left-brain test" below to better understand this once-popular idea.

1. Right now, my living space is _____.
  a. a big mess   **b.** fairly organized

[1]**intuitive:** based on feelings rather than facts
[2]**stability:** the condition of being strong, steady, and not changing

2. I _____ listen to music while I work.
  a. often   **b.** rarely

3. When I make a decision, I usually follow _____.
  a. my feelings   **b.** logic

4. I do a better job of remembering people's _____.
  a. faces   **b.** names

5. I get my best ideas when I am _____.
  a. lying down   **b.** standing up

6. This sentence best describes me.
  a. I like things to change.   **b.** I prefer things to stay the same.

7. In math, I can get the right answer, _____.
  a. and I can explain how I did it   **b.** but I cannot explain how I did it

4   If you had a majority of "A" answers, you were seen as a right brain-dominated thinker. If you answered more often with "B," then you were thought to be a left brain-dominated thinker. Your answers might have **indicated** that you were both creative *and* logical, or both artistic *and* good at math. Such people were considered a combination of the two types.

5   In the past, many scientists also thought that each of us **displayed** certain characteristics because one part of our brain dominated the other. The idea started with scientific study of the 1800s. Scientists found that an injury to one side of the brain caused a

loss of specific abilities. For example, spatial[3] abilities seemed to exist in the right side of the brain, with language in the left. Scientists then concluded that the two sides of the brain functioned independently.

6   But in today's scientific community, most experts now believe that the two sides of the brain do not work independently. Recent brain-scan[4] technology has **revealed** that the roles of each side of the brain are, in fact, complementary.[5] Scientists like Joseph Hellige, a psychologist at the University of Southern California, now thinks that the two sides of the brain work together. Hellige found that language **processing**, once believed to occur only in the left side of the brain, actually takes place in both sides. The brain's left side processes grammar and pronunciation while the right side processes intonation.[6] Similarly, Hellige's experiments show that the right side of the brain does not work in isolation[7] regarding[8] spatial ability. The right side deals with a general sense of space, and the left deals with objects in specific locations.

7   Researchers are struggling to understand the mysteries of the brain and to separate its myths and facts. With time and technology, they will know more about how the brain affects individual differences in personality. For now, scientists conclude that the idea of right-brain or left-brain dominance is probably too simple to be true.

---

[3] **spatial:** the position, size, or shape of things
[4] **brain scan:** an imaging method for finding problems in the brain
[5] **complementary:** needed to make something complete

---

[6] **intonation:** the rise and fall in the level of your voice
[7] **in isolation:** separately
[8] **regarding:** concerning

Identifying Main Ideas

Read each question. Circle the letter of the best answer.

1. What is the writer's main idea about right-brain and left-brain dominance?
   a. It was once a common belief.
   b. It is most likely a myth.
   c. It affects personality.
   d. It occurs in all individuals.

2. What conclusion does the writer make about the theory of right-brain, left-brain dominance in paragraphs 5 and 6?
   a. It was based on scientific research studies of the 1800s.
   b. It stated that both sides of the brain operated independently.
   c. It suggested that language was processed in one side of the brain.
   d. It was once accepted but is no longer believed to be true.

3. What is the writer's main point in paragraph 7?
   a. Scientists are continuing to study how the brain works.
   b. Technology will help scientists better understand the brain.
   c. The brain causes individuals to behave differently.
   d. The right-brain, left-brain theory is very mysterious.

Identifying Details

Complete the chart below with the phrases from the box.

have messy living spaces	are creative and artistic
rarely listen to music at work	remember people's faces
do well in mathematics	make decisions logically

The characteristics formerly associated with . . .

LEFT BRAIN-DOMINANT THINKERS	RIGHT BRAIN-DOMINANT THINKERS
	have messy living spaces

Making Inferences

The answers to the questions are not directly stated in the reading. Infer what the writer would say is true. Circle the letter of the best answer.

1. What is the writer's main purpose in including a right-brain, left-brain test?
   a. to help readers discover if they are right- or left-brain thinkers
   b. to help explain the theory of right- and left-brain dominance

2. Paragraph 4 mentions that right-brain thinkers are logical, and left-brain thinkers are creative. What does this suggest about right- and left-brain thinkers?
   a. They have opposite personalities.
   b. They have similar personalities.

3. In paragraph 5, what does the writer suggest about scientific study of the 1800s?

   a. Scientists were careful to do enough research to support the theory.

   b. Scientists accepted the theory without doing enough research.

4. According to paragraph 7, what is likely *not* to happen in the future regarding studies of the brain?

   a. Scientists will accept the right-brain, left-brain theory.

   b. Scientists will continue to study how the brain works.

READING SKILL

Scanning a Reading

Scanning means reading something quickly to find a particular piece of information. When you scan, you often have a question in mind. For example, you may need to find the times for a movie in a newspaper or the location of a lunch meeting mentioned in an e-mail.

Here is a basic two-step strategy for effective scanning:

- **Identify key words.** Identify a key word or words related to your question. Choose the most important word(s) that will help you answer your question.

  EXAMPLE

  Question: Where is the meeting?

  Key words: *meeting, restaurant*

- **Do not read every word.** Keep your key word(s) in mind as you scan. Do not read every word. Instead, skip over unimportant words and use your key word(s) to quickly search for the answer to your question.

Practice

Scan the reading on pages 46–47 to find more descriptions of left-brain and right-brain thinking. Look for key words such as **left brain**, **right brain**, *and* **think/thinker/thinking**. *List those descriptions in a chart like the one at the left.*

Journal
Choose one
question and
write a journal
entry.

Reflecting on the Reading

Which qualities best describe your personality? Give examples of behavior.
Discuss your answers in pairs or small groups.

My Personal Qualities

ARE YOU . . .	YES	NO	EXAMPLE
creative?			
logical?			
disorganized?			
stable?			
artistic?			
emotional?			

Vocabulary
For more
practice with
vocabulary, go
to page 196.

Activating Your Vocabulary

Take notes on these questions. Try to use your answers in your Writing
Assignment.

1. Think of someone who is **creative**. How does this person show his or her creativity?
2. Do you know a **logical** person? What does this person do to **display** his or her sense of logic?
3. In what situations do you have trouble **processing** what people say? What helps you in these situations?
4. Why is it essential for all people to be **flexible**?
5. Do you think of **dominance** as a positive or a negative quality? Why?

Read the model essay.

Arlene's Personality

The moment you walk into Arlene's house, you can sense her personality. Her two-story home is filled with old wooden and stuffed furniture and interesting art on the walls and shelves. She lets her cats and dogs run freely, up on tables, counters, and chairs. All of this suggests Arlene's disorganized, artistic, and spontaneous personality.

Arlene admits that she is messy. In her living room, she leaves books and objects lying all around in baskets and bowls. It looks like she is constantly in motion. She starts one thing, gets interrupted, and then moves on to another. She sometimes has trouble finding her keys or her book bag in the confusion of the space. And yet she gets things done. She goes to school, feeds the pets, and deals with her essential responsibilities well. It's just that her *things* are always in a mess, though she doesn't seem to mind at all.

Arlene is also an artist at heart. The objects of art that she collects—jewelry, Oriental rugs, paintings, and ceramics—reflect her interest in artistic beauty. She appreciates art, and she applies her talent to the jewelry and pottery that she creates. Arlene also has other artistic talents. She plays the piano and the saxophone, and she often goes to concerts. Art plays an important role in her life.

Above all, Arlene is a very spontaneous person. This means that she does things without planning them. For instance, if she leaves her house in the morning to go food shopping, she may stop at a bookstore or at the movies. She is open to new ideas and new places, so her friends like to be around her. Arlene is an easy travel companion, too. If you're in a new place and pass by a museum or a park, she's always ready to explore even if the stop was not planned. She really enjoys doing surprising things.

Arlene has many friends, and not all of them share her qualities of being messy, artistic, and spontaneous. However, that makes her companions enjoy her company. It's often interesting to spend time with someone who is not just like you, especially someone as special as Arlene. She is a true artist—and that makes her an interesting person to know.

WRITING SKILL

Organizing an Expository Essay

An **expository essay** explains or analyzes a topic. A paragraph and an essay are organized in similar ways, with a main idea, body, and a conclusion.

Essay Organization

The model essay, "Arlene's Personality," is organized just like a paragraph, but on a larger scale.

- **Introduction with thesis statement:** Just as a paragraph has a topic sentence, an essay has a thesis statement in the introductory paragraph. Like a topic sentence, the thesis statement gives the main idea about the entire essay. The thesis statement also often states the supporting points that you will present in the body of the essay. This introductory paragraph usually starts with a few sentences to catch the reader's interest before the thesis statement is stated.
- **Body paragraphs with topic sentence and supporting points:** One or more supporting paragraphs make up the body of an essay. Each body paragraph makes a different point about the thesis, begins with its own topic sentence, and has supporting sentences.
- **Conclusion:** The concluding paragraph brings the essay to an end. It is often a short paragraph that includes one sentence that restates the main idea, or thesis, of the essay.

Practice

A. Look back at "Arlene's Personality." Identify each of these parts in that essay.

1. thesis statement _____

    _____

2. sentences that precede thesis statement to create interest (give one example) _____

    _____

3. topic sentence for a body paragraph (give one example) _____

    _____

4. sentence in conclusion that resates the thesis _____

    _____

> **Writing Checklist**
>
> ❏ Does your essay have an introduction paragraph?
>
> ❏ Does your introduction include a thesis statement that states your main idea?
>
> ❏ Does each of your body paragraphs include one supporting point about the topic?
>
> ❏ Did you include at least two examples in each body paragraph?
>
> ❏ Did you end your essay with a concluding paragraph that restates the main idea?
>
> ❏ Did you use vocabulary from the chapter appropriately?

STEP 5 **Edit your writing.**

  A. Edit your essay. Correct any mistakes in capitalization, punctuation, spelling, or verb use.

  B. Exchange essays with a partner. Use the Correction Symbols on page 191 to mark each other's work.

  EXAMPLE

  SUBJECT-VERB AGREEMENT ERROR (agr)

  spends
  My math professor ~~spend~~ many hours helping his students.

STEP 6 **Write a final copy.**

  Correct your mistakes. Copy your final essay and give it to your instructor.

Artists as Scientists and Entrepreneurs

Ray and Charles Eames, 1960

PRE-READING

Discussion

Discuss the questions in pairs or small groups.

1. Look at the photograph. By definition, artists "produce or perform any type of art such as painting, music, dance, etc." What type of art do you think Ray and Charles Eames produced?

2. The title of the reading is "Artists as Scientists and Businesspeople." Why does an artist need to know about science or business?

3. Think of an artist that you like—a painter, musician, singer, dancer, or actor. Does this person also have skills in science or in entrepreneurship (starting a business)? Explain.

Vocabulary

Read the sentences. Match the boldfaced words with the definitions.

_b_   1. Charles and Ray Eames were well-known furniture **designers**. They worked together to create new styles of chairs.

____   2. One **technique** that the Eameses used was to make chairs from single pieces of wood. This made their chairs look modern, simple, and useful.

____   3. They **incorporated** their knowledge of science into their art. Top scientists helped them improve the ways they built furniture.

____   4. In addition, their skills in business **enabled** them to succeed in the art world. Their chairs are still popular today.

____   5. The Eameses had many **diverse** interests. They were known not only for making furniture but also for building houses, photography, and other art forms.

____   6. They **experimented** with different ways to put the pieces of their furniture together. They were among the first people to use heat to help connect the parts of their chairs.

____   7. All of the Eameses' art **represents** their central ideas about art. They thought art should be modern, useful, and attractive.

____   8. Charles and Ray Eames were **extraordinary** artists. They were well-known as two of the top artists of the 20th century.

---

a. very different from each other
b. people who make drawings or plans of something that will be made or built
c. make it possible for someone or something to do something
d. show or mean a thing or idea
e. a special way of doing something
f. try using various ideas, methods, or materials in order to find out how effective or good they are
g. include something as part of a group, system, etc.
h. very unusual, special, or surprising

Artists as Scientists and Entrepreneurs

1   Charles and Ray Eames are among the best-known **designers** of the 20th century. Together, this husband-and-wife team mastered many **diverse** art forms including furniture design, architecture, painting, and photography. At heart, they were artists, yet their skills in science and business also **enabled** them to succeed in the design world.

2   It is clear that the Eameses had a great deal of artistic talent. In 1946, they produced "the most talked-about chairs of the year," according to *House & Garden* magazine. These "chairs for tomorrow" were displayed at the Museum of Modern Art in New York City. The Eameses' chairs were fresh, new, and affordable[1]— $11 to $16. These chairs are still popular today. In addition to chairs, the couple also designed inexpensive, practical houses. Their own Eames House looked like a large, square box with wooden, steel, and glass sections. It had clean, simple lines, with large windows, sliding doors, and airy interior spaces. All of the Eameses' work **represented** their central idea about design. They made things that were modern and useful but attractive.

3   As well as being attractive, their designs also indicate their strong interest in science. The couple worked with top scientists to create products that met their own high technical standards. For instance, they created new manufacturing methods. They connected chair parts with heat and glue, a **technique** called "electronic bonding." They also used rubber to join the backs and seats of their chairs to distribute[2] the weight of the user. Furthermore, they **experimented** with ways to make chairs, tables, and other furniture out of single pieces of wood, fiberglass,[3] plastic, or metal. Another particular interest of Charles Eames was the TV show called *Mathematica*. He and his wife are shown working in this show in 1960 in the photograph on page 56. Charles Eames created this show to help people understand mathematical and scientific ideas by viewing everyday objects. This artistic team **incorporated** science into their art in a variety of ways.

4   They also used successful business practices. From 1943 to 1988, the Eames Office near Los Angeles served as a large

[1] **affordable:** not expensive

[2] **distribute:** to spread throughout a given area
[3] **fiberglass:** a light material made from small fibers (threads) of glass

workshop. Teams of artists produced furniture, photographs, and paintings for customers. In all of their work, the couple was guided by a strong customer focus. "Early in their careers together, Charles and Ray identified the need for affordable, yet high-quality furniture for the average consumer[4]—furniture that could serve a variety of uses," according to the U.S. Library of Congress. Two manufacturing companies sold the couple's chairs, storage units, and benches[5]

[4] **consumer:** someone who buys or uses goods or services
[5] **benches:** long seats for two or more people

around the world. Their furniture had strong sales beginning in the mid-20th century and still sells well today.

5   Charles and Ray Eames were **extraordinary** artists. They remind us of Leonardo da Vinci, who painted the *Mona Lisa* while he studied nature and aeronautics.[6] Da Vinci started out poor but ended his career in the 1500s under the financial support of a French king. Like Leonardo da Vinci, Charles and Ray Eames used their science and business talents to help them create beautiful art.

[6] **aeronautics:** the science or art of flight

Identifying Main Ideas

Match each paragraph with its main idea.

_____ 1. paragraph 1
_____ 2. paragraph 2
_____ 3. paragraph 3
_____ 4. paragraph 4

a. The Eameses used science to create their products.

b. The Eameses are famous designers of the 20th century.

c. The Eameses were talented artists.

d. The Eameses succeeded because their ideas focused on customer needs.

Identifying Details

Match the dates on the left with the events on the right.

_____ 1. 1500s
_____ 2. 1943
_____ 3. 1946
_____ 4. 1960
_____ 5. 20th century

a. Da Vinci was supported by a French king.

b. Charles Eames worked in a mathematics show.

c. The Eameses were well-known designers.

d. The Eameses' workshop opened in Los Angeles.

e. The team produced the first Eames chairs.

Making Inferences

What meaning can be inferred from the sentence? Circle the letter of the best answer.

1. At heart, they were artists, yet their skills in science and business also enabled them to succeed in the design world.
   a. The Eameses were artists first, and scientists and businesspeople second.
   b. The Eameses used their emotions to create their artistic designs.

2. Another particular interest of Charles Eames was the TV show called *Mathematica.*
   a. The writer wants to show that Charles Eames was interested in shows.
   b. The writer wants to show that Charles Eames was interested in science.

3. They remind us of Leonardo da Vinci, who painted the *Mona Lisa* while he studied nature and aeronautics.
   a. The writer is emphasizing that da Vinci was interested in both art and science.
   b. The writer is emphasizing that da Vinci was best known as the man who painted the *Mona Lisa.*

FROM READING TO WRITING

Journal
Choose one question and write a journal entry.

Reflecting on the Reading

Discuss the questions in pairs or small groups.

1. The Eameses were successful artists because of their skills in art, science, and business. How did their knowledge of science and business contribute to their success?
2. Imagine that you want to have a career as an artist. What should you do to become successful?
3. Would you be more interested in becoming an artist, a scientist, or a businessperson? Explain.

Activating Your Vocabulary

Take notes on these questions. Try to use your answers in your Writing Assignment.

1. Think of someone who is a **designer**. What does he or she design?
2. What skills **enable** an artist to create art?
3. Think of someone who is intelligent. How does that person **incorporate** business skills into his or her life?
4. What is one **technique** a businessperson would use to become successful?
5. Think of what a scientist does. What might that person **experiment** with?

WRITING

**WRITING
SKILL**

Writing an Effective Thesis Statement

The thesis statement tells the reader the main idea of the essay. In addition, the thesis statement often provides a "road map" that tells what supporting points will appear in the body paragraphs of the essay.

EXAMPLE

Thesis Statement

SUPPORTING POINTS

               1   2   3

At heart, they were **artists**, yet their skills in **science** and **business** also enabled them to succeed in the design world.

Supporting point 1:

It is clear that the Eameses had a great deal of <u>artistic talent</u>.

Supporting point 2:

As well as being attractive, their designs also indicate their strong interest in <u>science</u>.

Supporting point 3:

They also used successful <u>business</u> practices.

Follow these guidelines to write an effective thesis statement:
- **Make your thesis statement clear and specific.** The first thesis statement below is too general, but the second one is clearer and more specific.

Less effective: My aunt is a successful business owner.

Effective: My aunt is a successful business owner because she has several positive qualities.

- **Do not merely announce the topic in your thesis statement.**
  Phrases such as *I will write about* . . . announce the topic but add no useful information.

Less effective:	In this essay, I will discuss two qualities of the singer Sean Paul.
Effective:	Sean Paul uses creative beats and thoughtful lyrics in his songs.

- **Do not include the word *I* in your thesis statement.**

Less effective:	I feel that my friend Richard has contrasting characteristics.
Effective:	My friend Richard has contrasting characteristics.

Practice

A. Which of these thesis statements are effective? Write E (Effective). Rewrite the other thesis statements to make them more effective.

_____ 1. This essay will describe my sister Diana's characteristics.

     My sister Diana is a cheerful and caring person.

_____ 2. Dr. Woodford is a pleasant and competent physician.

     . _____

_____ 3. My brother Hun has a money-making pizza shop.

     _____

_____ 4. Unfortunately, my friend Anna has some very negative qualities.

     _____

_____ 5. I believe that my father has many good qualities.

     _____

B. Work in pairs. Write other possible topic sentences for body paragraphs to support these thesis statements. Discuss your answers.

1. Thesis statement: My mother is a cheerful and loving person.

   Body paragraph 1: *She is always in a good mood.*

   Body paragraph 2: _____

2. Thesis statement: My boss is hard but fair with her employees.

   Body paragraph 1: *She pushes us to do the best we can.*

   Body paragraph 2: _____

3. Thesis statement: My boyfriend, Mike, is even-tempered and respectful.

Body paragraph 1: _____

Body paragraph 2: *Also, he respects others.* _____

C. **Choose a topic from Exercise B. Work in pairs. Make notes about examples to include in each body paragraph.**

WRITING ASSIGNMENT

Write an essay. Follow the steps.

STEP 1 **Get ideas.**

A. Choose a topic for your essay. Check (✔) it.

☐ **Topic 1:** The skills or interests of an artist.

☐ **Topic 2:** The skills or interests of a scientist.

☐ **Topic 3:** The skills or interests of a businessperson.

B. Work in groups. Brainstorm names of people who have those specific skills or interests.

C. Choose one person from your list as the subject of your essay. Make a chart like the one below.

Person: *Leonardo da Vinci*

IDENTIFICATION OF PERSON	*master painter* *painted the Mona Lisa*
1ST SKILL OR INTEREST	*plants*
2ND SKILL OR INTEREST	*the body*

D. Add examples that explain each skill or interest area.

STEP 2   Organize your ideas.

Use the information below to organize your essay.

- **Introduction** Introduce the person that you are writing about. End the introductory paragraph with a thesis statement that states the person's skills or interest areas.

    EXAMPLES

    Topic 1: Jennifer Lopez' determination and business sense have helped her become a success.

    Topic 3: My father and uncle have a successful business because they are energetic, well-organized, and cooperative.

- **Body paragraph 1** Begin with a topic sentence about the person's first skill or interest area. Use your notes from Step 1. Include at least two examples that explain this point.

- **Body paragraph 2** Begin with a topic sentence about the person's second skill or interest area. Include at least two examples that explain this point.

- **Body paragraph 3** If you include a third supporting point, begin with a topic sentence about this skill or interest area. Include at least two examples that explain this point.

- **Conclusion** Write a concluding paragraph that restates the main idea in different words.

STEP 3   Write a rough draft.

Write your essay. Use the information from Steps 1 and 2. Include vocabulary from the chapter where possible.

STEP 4   Revise your rough draft.

Read your paragraph. Use the Writing Checklist to look for mistakes. Work alone or in pairs.

Writing Checklist

- ❑ Does your introduction include an effective thesis statement?
- ❑ Does each body paragraph have a topic sentence that explains more about the thesis statement?
- ❑ Did you include examples in the body paragraphs to explain the main ideas?
- ❑ Did you end your essay with a conclusion that restates the main idea?
- ❑ Did you use correct essay format, such as adding a title and indenting the first line of each paragraph?
- ❑ Did you use vocabulary from the chapter appropriately?

STEP 5 **Edit your writing.**

A. Edit your essay. Correct any mistakes in capitalization, punctuation, spelling, or verb use.

B. Exchange essays with a partner. Use the Correction Symbols on page 191 to mark each other's work.

EXAMPLE

SUBJECT-VERB AGREEMENT ERROR (agr)

speaks
The pop singer Shakira ~~speak~~ three languages.

STEP 6 **Write a final copy.**

Correct your mistakes. Copy your final paragraph and give it to your instructor.

UNIT FOUR

Leisure

The Art of Paintball

**In this chapter
you will:**

• read an article
about how to
play the sport of
paintball

• learn strategies
for recognizing
repetition of
ideas

• write an
introduction for
a process essay

A paintball player with equipment

PRE-READING

Discussion

Discuss the questions in pairs or small groups.

1. Look at the photograph. Paintball is an *extreme*, or action, sport. Have you heard of this sport? What do you know about it?
2. Paintball is a physically and mentally challenging sport. Would you enjoy playing this sport? Explain.
3. Imagine that you have money and a free weekend. What would you do? Where would you go?

Vocabulary

Circle the letter of the word or phrase that is NOT close in meaning to the boldfaced word.

1. There was a feeling of **anticipation** before our college basketball team started its final game of the year. Everyone was waiting for the action to begin.

    a. expectation   b. eagerness   (c.) worry

2. The **opposing** team had very strong players, but our team performed better.

    a. united   b. opposite   c. competing

3. An important **element** in the game was the weather. Even though it was hot and humid, our athletes scored very well.

    a. factor   b. part   c. result

4. One **aim** of basketball is to get control of the ball, and our players succeeded in taking the ball away from the opponents many times.

    a. effect   b. purpose   c. goal

5. Our team used their strongest players in the front of the court. This **strategy** prevented the other team from scoring.

    a. plan   b. approach   c. disorder

6. One of the **features** of our college gymnasium is that it has large sections of movable seats.

    a. changes   b. benefits   c. characteristics

7. My friends and I **take advantage of** our free time by shooting baskets in the gym.

    a. profit from   b. make use of   c. treat badly

8. Playing basketball well **involves** using your leg and arm muscles.

    a. includes   b. concerns   c. affects

9. The team won a city-wide **match** by defeating another neighboring school.

    a. teamwork   b. competition   c. contest

The Art of Paintball

1   Deep in the woods, groups of men, women, and children dressed in camouflage[1] clothing wait impatiently on wooden benches. There's a sense of **anticipation** in the air. Everyone is getting ready to play—loading plastic paintballs into toy guns, checking their clothing, and tying colored pieces of cloth onto their arms. One group of players looks around nervously at another group seated nearby. Then a referee[2] shouts, "Brown! Green!" and the two groups move out onto a dirt path. Goggles in place over their eyes, they enter a wooded field where they will face their opponents in a fast-moving, competitive **match**. Do you imagine yourself in this group? If so, then these basics may help you decide whether you want to play the action sport of paintball.

2   First, you should understand your assignment. Basically, paintball is a team sport in which players work together to capture, or catch, an **opposing** team's flag. It's like the children's game of "capture the flag," but with the added **element** of paintballs. Opponents attempt to hit each other with paintballs— small plastic balls filled with paint—that are propelled[3] from plastic or metal toy guns, called "markers." The markers have carbon dioxide[4] or helium[5]-filled tanks attached.

Being hit by a paintball doesn't hurt much. It just leaves washable paint on your clothing. The **aim** is to hit, but not *be hit* since once a player is hit, he or she must leave the field. The first team to capture the flag from the opposing team and return it to their side wins, and the match ends.

3   If this sounds like child's play, consider the elements of physical fitness and mental **strategy** involved. You must be in good shape to play the sport well. Paintball requires running, diving, sliding, crawling, and holding the marker in position for long periods of time. To prepare, you should do exercises like running or bicycling to build overall body strength and lift weights to build arm muscles. The game also requires stealth,[6] so those who preview the field to learn about the **features** of the land are more likely to succeed. It's a game of mental strategy, too—knowing how to hide from opponents, how to show your body in order to attack, and how to reach the opponent's flag safely. These physical and mental actions must be performed within a team, so successful players **take advantage of** their own and their teammates' strengths.

4   The most important skill required is "snap-shooting"—being able to show yourself for only a few seconds as you fire paintballs from behind a rock or tree and then quickly snap your body back behind the cover. Many first-timers make the mistake of looking out from behind the tree or other cover for too

[1]**camouflage:** the things you use to hide something by making it look the same as the things around it
[2]**referee:** someone who makes sure that the rules are followed during a game in sports
[3]**propel:** to move, drive, or push something forward
[4]**carbon dioxide:** the gas produced when animals breathe out
[5]**helium:** a gas that is lighter than air

[6]**stealth:** the action of doing something quietly and secretly

long. Players must always have their eyes and heads covered, and shoot opponents only below their waists. But the trick is to show as little of your body as possible while still shooting paintballs. In other words, keep yourself hidden, take quick peeks to see the opponent, and don't open yourself up to[7] being hit.

5   Of course, no one can play without paying, and paintball is a relatively expensive sport. A one-day outing can cost us $200 or more, considering that you will probably shoot 1,000 to 2,000 paintballs in eight to ten matches. There's also the expense of an entry fee to a private field and the rental of the gun and any extra equipment you desire, such as

knee or elbow pads, cases for storing extra paintballs, and sweat-free goggles. Also, you must dress appropriately. In wooded paintball fields, you need camouflage-colored clothing and high-top boots to avoid ankle injuries. These expenses do not concern serious paintball players, however. Many of them spend thousands of dollars on their own equipment and clothing.

6   While paintball may be too active for some people, it's fairly safe. According to *Splat!* magazine, paintball is safer than any other action sport, and it's even safer than tennis or golf. The supporters of the sport stress that, in the end, paintball is simply a game. It's a challenging sport, but it also **involves** team play in a natural setting. Perhaps one day you may join the millions of players who make paintball one of the most popular extreme sports in the world.

----

[7] **open yourself up to:** show yourself so that something might happen to you

Identifying Main Ideas

Match the beginning of each sentence with an ending. Then circle the number of the sentence that represents the main idea of the reading.

_____ 1. In paintball, team members try to

_____ 2. Learning the basics of paintball can help you

_____ 3. Because paintball requires physical activity,

_____ 4. While shooting paintballs,

_____ 5. You need to pay for special clothing and an entry fee, so

a. you must be in good shape to play well.

b. you should try to show yourself for only a few seconds.

c. decide if you want to play this sport.

d. capture the flag of the opposing team.

e. paintball can be an expensive sport.

Identifying Details

Scan the reading. Complete the sentences with the missing details.

1. Before the game begins, everyone ties _____ pieces of cloth onto their _____.

2. Opponents try to hit each other with paintballs. Paintballs are _____ balls filled with _____.

3. The balls are propelled from guns made of _____ or _____. The guns are called _____.

4. Paintball players must wear the right clothing. In wooded paintball fields, they need _____ clothing and _____ boots to avoid injuries.

5. One day of paintball can cost _____.

6. In one day, a paintballer usually plays between _____ and _____ matches and shoots _____ to _____ paintballs.

Making Inferences

What meaning can be inferred from the sentence? Circle the letter of the best answer.

1. One group of players looks around nervously at another group seated nearby.
   a. One group of players is thinking of how to make friends with the other group.
   b. One group of players is thinking about how well the other group will play.

2. If this sounds like child's play, consider the elements of physical fitness and mental strategy involved.
   a. Paintball is an appropriate game for children.
   b. Paintball is not as easy to play as you think.

3. Many first-timers make the mistake of looking out from behind the tree or other cover for too long.
   a. If you look out from behind a tree, you will not get experience.
   b. If you look out for too long, you will be hit by a paintball.

READING SKILL

Recognizing Repetition of Ideas

Writers often use **repetition** to emphasize an important idea. Repetition is the writer's way of making sure that the main idea is understood and remembered. They may repeat complete sentences or parts of sentences. These repetitions often appear in the sentence following the topic sentence or at the end of a paragraph. Study the underlined repetitions in this paragraph from "The Art of Paintball."

> (1) If this sounds like child's play, consider the elements of <u>physical fitness and mental strategy involved</u>. (2) <u>You must be in good shape to play the sport well.</u> (3) Paintball requires running, diving, sliding, crawling, and holding the marker in position for long periods of time. (4) To prepare, you should do exercises like running or bicycling to build overall body strength and lift weights to build arm muscles. (5) The game also requires stealth, so those who preview the field to know the features of the land are more likely to succeed. (6) <u>It's a game of mental strategy</u>, too—knowing how to hide from opponents, how to show your body in order to attack, and how to reach the opponent's flag safely. (7) <u>These physical and mental actions must be performed</u> within a team, so successful players take advantage of their own and their teammates' strengths.

- **Emphatic sentences** Sentence 1 (the topic sentence) states the writer's main idea. Notice how sentences 2 and 6 emphasize an important idea from sentence 1. Sentence 2 does not add new information. Instead, it restates a part of the main idea in different words. The phrases *physical fitness* and *in good shape* repeat ideas. In sentence 6, the writer again restates a part of the main idea with the phrase *mental strategy*.
- **Concluding sentence** Notice how sentence 7 repeats the main idea. Again, the writer emphasizes the main idea by repeating it in different words. In the concluding sentence, the writer uses the phrase *physical and mental actions* to repeat the main idea from the topic sentence (*physical fitness and mental strategy.*)

Practice

Read paragraphs 5 and 6 of "The Art of Paintball" again. Then work in pairs and answer the questions.

Paragraph 5
1. What is the main idea? _____
2. What is the sentence or sentence part that repeats this idea? Underline it.
3. What is the sentence or sentence part that concludes the paragraph by repeating the main idea? Underline it.

Paragraph 6

1. What is the main idea?

   _____

2. What is the sentence or sentence part that repeats this idea? Underline it.

FROM READING TO WRITING

Journal
Choose one
topic and write
a journal entry.

Reflecting on the Reading

Complete the chart. List sports or games that illustrate each characteristic. Discuss your answers in pairs or small groups.

Characteristics of Sports or Games

CHARACTERISTIC	SPORT OR GAME
fast-moving	*soccer, basketball*
team sport	
requires physical fitness	
requires mental strategy	
expensive	
fairly safe	
challenging	

Vocabulary
For more
practice with
vocabulary, go
to page 198.

Activating Your Vocabulary

Think of a competitive sport and a leisure activity. Then take notes on these questions. Try to use your answers in your Writing Assignment.

1. What is the **aim** of the sport?
2. What is the main **strategy** that players must use against an **opposing** team?
3. What are the **features** of the place in which the leisure activity takes place?
4. What do you **anticipate** most about that leisure activity?
5. What **elements** of this sport or leisure activity do you enjoy the most? What **elements** do you dislike?

Read the model essay.

MODEL

Playing Sudoku

The game of *sudoku*, pronounced soo-doe-koo, is quickly becoming the fastest-growing puzzle in the world. It may look like a number game that requires only pencil, paper, and a little time, but it's not so simple. Here are the ways to play sudoku, an ancient game with different forms to challenge players of all ages.

The name *sudoku* is Japanese (*su* means "number," and *doku* means "singular," or "unique"). It seems fairly simple to play the modern version. You start with 81 squares divided into nine sections. Some squares have numbers in them. Enter a number from 1 through 9 in each empty square. Before you write, however, think carefully. Make sure that each row, column, *and* section of the grid contains only one instance of the number that you write. Your aim is to fill in each square with the correct number.

The sudoku may look like a mathematical puzzle, but it's actually a game of logic. Always use a pencil and be ready to do a lot of erasing. You need to test which numbers will work and take your time. Sudoku makers say that a typical game takes 10 to 30 minutes, but sometimes you get stuck. The time to finish depends on your skill and experience. There's no math involved, but you need patience and the ability to think logically.

Sudoku comes in various forms. The most common form is the nine by nine-square form illustrated above. However, there are sudokus for all ages and skill levels. Four by four sudokus are easier for children. Adult sudokus come in different sizes—even 25 by 25 squares. Most people play sudokus in books and newspapers, but you can also play them on a computer, a cell phone, or in board games. There are also graphic versions with photographs or drawings. In addition, there are sudokus with letters or symbols.

Sudoku is not the ideal leisure-time activity for everyone, but if you like a mental challenge, try it. You might agree with sudoku lovers that this little puzzle is making the world smarter.

Writing an Introduction for a Process Essay

An effective introductory paragraph for an essay has four basic features:
- It introduces the topic.
- It suggests how the writer will present the process in the essay.
- It contains the thesis statement.
- It catches the reader's interest.

Study the first paragraph of "Playing Sudoku." Does it have the four features?

The most common type of introduction is called the **funnel**. It is called a funnel because its ideas look like a funnel, progressing from the general (wide) to the specific (narrow). Here's how to organize a funnel introduction:

- **Begin with a general sentence that includes the topic word.** The first sentence is a general statement that contains a key word or words to introduce the topic.

    EXAMPLE

    The game of **sudoku**, pronounced soo-doe-koo, is quickly becoming the **fastest-growing puzzle** in the world.

    The key words are *sudoku* and *fastest-growing puzzle* in the world.

- **Include one or more sentences that become progressively more specific.** These sentences should connect the very general first sentence with the most specific sentence—the thesis statement.

    EXAMPLE

    It may look like a number game that requires only pencil, paper, and a little time, but it's not so simple.

    In this sentence, the phrase *it's not so simple* connects the general introductory sentence with the specific thesis statement, which focuses on the process of playing sudoku.

- **End with the thesis statement.** The last sentence of the introduction, the most specific statement, is the thesis of the essay. Repeat the key word or words about the topic, or include a synonym for the word, in the thesis. For a process essay (an essay that explains how to do something), your thesis statement should introduce the activity. It could also include words such as *process, steps, basics, guidelines, ways (to do something),* or *tips* so that it is clear that your essay will explain how to do something.

    EXAMPLE

    Here are the **ways** to **play sudoku**, an ancient game with different forms to challenge players of all ages.

    The restated ideas are *sudoku* and *challenge players of all ages.*

Practice

A. Read the introductory paragraphs. Underline the word or words that appear in the first sentence and are repeated in the thesis statement.

Paragraph 1

Smart Shopping on eBay

In this computer age, many shoppers turn to online stores like eBay to save money or find hard-to-find items. Not everyone has had good experiences with online shopping, though. Poor-quality products and high prices exist in every store, even online, so it's important to shop wisely. If you want to get your money's worth every time you buy an item on eBay, use these important strategies.

Paragraph 2

Tips for Snorkeling

Snorkeling stands out among many water sports. It's neither as simple as swimming nor as difficult as scuba diving. It's suitable for both children and adults, and it's an enjoyable way to view underwater life in a variety of bodies of water—rivers, lakes, or oceans. Indeed, the sport of snorkeling is an ideal water sport. If you can swim underwater, all you need to snorkel is inexpensive equipment and the right place.

B. Do the paragraphs in Exercise A have the four features of a process essay introduction discussed on the previous page? Discuss the features of each introduction in pairs or small groups.

C. Write an introduction for one of these thesis statements. Begin with a general sentence, add more specific sentences, and end with the thesis statement.

Thesis statement 1: Before you start an exercise program, consider these simple guidelines.
Thesis statement 2: Planning a vacation takes careful preparation.
Thesis statement 3: Digital photography is a useful skill that's easy to learn.

_____

_____

_____

_____

_____

_____

_____

D. Work in groups. Discuss your introductions. Does each contain the four basic features of a good introduction?

WRITING ASSIGNMENT

Write an introduction for a process essay. Follow the steps.

STEP 1   Get ideas.

    A. Choose a sport, game, or other leisure-time activity that you enjoy.

    B. In groups, explain the activity.

    C. Choose a topic for your essay introduction. Check (✔) it.

    ❑ **Topic 1:** How to play a sport or game

    ❑ **Topic 2:** How to do a leisure-time activity

    D. Write an effective thesis statement for your topic.

        EXAMPLE

        Topic 2:   Making tamales is a time-consuming yet simple process if you follow these steps.

    E. Show your thesis statement to your instructor before you continue.

STEP 2   Organize your ideas.

Use the steps in writing a funnel introduction presented on page 76. You will finish writing the essay in the next chapter.

STEP 3   Write a rough draft.

Write your introduction. Include vocabulary from the chapter where possible.

STEP 4   Revise your rough draft.

Read your paragraph. Use the Writing Checklist to look for mistakes. Work alone or in pairs.

Writing Checklist

❑ Does your paragraph introduce the topic?

❑ Does it say how you will develop your topic?

❑ Does it try to catch the reader's interest?

❑ Did you include key words about the topic in the thesis statement and make it clear that the essay will discuss how to do something?

❑ Did you include repetition of ideas?

❑ Did you use vocabulary from the chapter appropriately?

STEP 5   Edit your writing

    A. Edit your paragraph. Correct any mistakes in capitalization, punctuation, spelling, or verb use.

    B. Exchange paragraphs with a partner. Use the Correction Symbols on page 191 to mark each other's work.

    EXAMPLE

PUNCTUATION ERROR (**P**)

because

Playing a musical instrument is not simple. ~~Because~~ it takes time.

STEP 6   Write a final copy.

Correct your mistakes. Copy your final paragraph and give it to your instructor.

Camping in Oz

*In this chapter
you will:*

• read an essay
about camping
in Australia

• learn how to
write a
concluding
paragraph

• organize and
write a process
essay

Visitors to Kakadu National Park in Australia

PRE-READING

Discussion

Discuss the questions in pairs or small groups.

1. Look at the photograph of a park in Australia. This huge country, often called *Oz*, has many types of natural landscapes. Which of the following places in nature have you seen? Describe them.

   cave   cliff   desert   table rock   waterfall

2. Do you enjoy spending time in nature? Why or why not?

3. In your opinion, is going camping an enjoyable vacation? Explain.

Vocabulary

Read the sentences. Match the boldfaced words with the definitions.

__c__ 1. Some researchers say that air travel is bad for the **environment** because airplanes generate a lot of pollution.

____ 2. Do you prefer to go to the movies alone or with **companions**?

____ 3. The **site** where I set up my telescope was perfect for viewing the stars.

____ 4. Let's **arrange** our schedules so that we can play basketball together every Tuesday afternoon.

____ 5. Shopping malls have many stores **concentrated** in a small area. All the stores are located in one building.

____ 6. The zoo opens at 9:00 A.M. Luckily, I bought my tickets **ahead of time**, so I can walk right in as soon as the gates open.

____ 7. After a day at the beach, most people use the showers or other **facilities** for washing off sand and sea water.

____ 8. I'll arrive at 1:00 P.M. tomorrow if I make the early morning train. If I miss the first train, I'll arrive at 3:00 P.M. **In any event**, I'll be there tomorrow.

____ 9. I left my keys in the gymnasium, but **luckily** they were still there when I went back for them.

____ 10. Even though it's more **economical** to take a bus than a train, some people would rather pay more for the comfort of a train.

---

a. someone you spend a lot of time with
b. whatever happens or whatever situation
c. the land, water, and air in which people, animals, and plants live
d. before an event or a particular time
e. to be present in large numbers or amounts in a particular place
f. happily, fortunately
g. rooms, equipment, or services that are provided for a particular purpose
h. a place where something interesting or important happens
i. using time, money, or products without waste
j. make plans for something to happen

Camping in Oz

1   Every year, millions of visitors flock[1] to Kakadu National Park in northern Australia to view the unique rocks, waterfalls, wildlife, and ancient rock art of this vast[2] 20,000-square-kilometer park. There's so much to see and do that many visitors stay there overnight. They can walk, hike, climb, animal-watch, or just be lazy. Camping in a natural **environment** involves much more than simply putting up a tent, however. Like elsewhere,[3] camping in Australia requires careful planning and preparation.

2   First, it requires choosing from a variety of natural places. Australia is the world's sixth largest country, and it has mountains, deserts, forests, oceans, beaches, rivers, and other natural features. In fact, many areas offer a blend of natural settings. Royal National Park in Victoria, near Sydney, has a river, beach, and rain forest with waterfalls. The Bungonia State Conservation Area in southeastern Australia has mountain caves, cliffs, and table rocks for campers who are willing to bring their own water and hike to their campsite. Indeed, Australia is so vast that campers really have to do their homework.[4] Photographs and articles in books and on the Internet can describe the landscapes and wildlife of each region. Local residents can also share their experiences, especially if they have lived in the area for a long time. All this research can uncover unusual places or travel **companions** who may ask if they can come along!

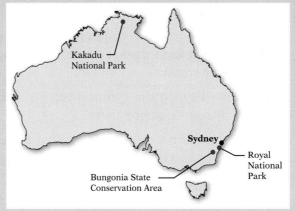

Kakadu National Park

Sydney

Royal National Park

Bungonia State Conservation Area

3   Of course, time and money are also important considerations. The good thing about camping in Australia is that it's inexpensive. Most state and national parks charge AU$7 per vehicle (about US$6) to enter a park and AU$5 (about US$4) per adult camper per night. The difficult thing, however, is that Australia is so huge that it challenges visitors with limited time. Campers with only a few days' vacation have to choose **sites** close to their homes, or **arrange** their travel so that they stay in parks that are **concentrated** in one state or region. **Luckily**, the country and its surrounding islands are full of state and national parks and private campgrounds. Some tour companies, like Oz Experience, cater to[5] campers and backpackers by providing **economical** bus trips that take tourists from park to park.

4   Once a campground is selected, campers should reserve places **ahead of time** to get a

---

[1] **flock:** When people *flock* to a place, a lot of them go there.
[2] **vast:** extremely large
[3] **elsewhere:** in another place
[4] **do their homework:** idiom — to learn everything people need to know before doing something

[5] **cater to:** provide a particular group of people with something that they need or want

good location. Even at less crowded state parks, campers need to make campsite reservations a week or a few days in advance. Popular parks like the Kakadu National Park require reservations months in advance. When making reservations, campers should keep these questions in mind: Is the site located in the most beautiful area of the park? Is it near a river, lake, or ocean? Does it have running water and other facilities? Does it permit pets? Again, the Internet will make it easier to choose the exact campsite. Websites often include photographs and campground maps, and many allow visitors to make online reservations.

5   The next step is preparing what to take, which can be a time-consuming part of planning the trip. Basically, campers will need something to sleep in and on, food, cooking equipment, lighting equipment, and clothing. Here, again, money is an important point.

Camping can be an expensive pastime, so travelers should decide how much money they want to spend on gear like a backpack, tent, sleeping bags, flashlights, or cookware. Friends or second-hand stores may be sources for cheaper camping gear. Another factor is weight. If campers plan to carry all their goods in a backpack, then these items must be light. How-to books or websites can give travelers ideas about the variety of gear that is available for different camping situations. In any event, campers will find that it takes time to gather the items that they choose to bring.

6   Preparing for a camping trip may seem like a great deal of work, but in the end the reward will be the joy of spending time in the wild. Why should nature lovers pay to sleep in hotels? With a little luck and favorable weather, there's no better way than camping to see natural beauty and wildlife up close.

Identifying Main Ideas

Read each question. Circle the letter of the best answer.

1. Which of the following titles best expresses the main idea of the reading?
   a. How to Save Money on Camping in Australia
   b. Where to Find a Campsite in Australia
   c. How to Plan a Camping Trip in Australia
   d. How to Decide What to Take Camping in Australia

2. What is the writer's main advice to campers in paragraph 2?
   a. They should ask local residents for information.
   b. They may need to hike and carry water at campsites.
   c. They should read books to find out about campsites.
   d. They must do research to choose a camping place.

3. In paragraph 3, what is the writer's main purpose?
   a. to urge people to think about time and money
   b. to warn people to be prepared about costs
   c. to describe the size of Australia
   d. to explain the typical costs of camping

4. What is the writer's main point about camping gear in paragraph 5?

   a. It's expensive.

   b. It's available online.

   c. It takes time to choose.

   d. It should be lightweight.

5. What is the best description for the reading?

   a. an essay that argues in favor of camping trips

   b. a study that compares different camping places

   c. an article that explains how to plan a camping trip

   d. a narrative story about one camping vacation

Identifying Details

Scan the reading. Find these features or places. Check (✔) the ones that describe each place.

PLACE	FEATURES				
	rocks	beaches	waterfalls	caves	mountains
Kakadu National Park					
Royal National Park					
Bungonia State Conservation Area					

Making Inferences

What meaning can be inferred from the sentence? Circle the letter of the best answer.

1. The difficult thing, however, is that Australia is so huge that it challenges visitors with limited time.

   a. It takes a long time to travel from place to place in Australia.

   b. Australians do not have enough time to meet all the visitors.

2. Once a campground is selected, campers should reserve places ahead of time to get a good location.

   a. The best campgrounds should have reservation systems.

   b. The best campgrounds may be in high demand by campers.

3. Why should nature lovers pay to sleep in hotels?

   a. Nature lovers cannot afford hotels.

   b. Hotels do not offer an experience with nature.

4. With a little luck and favorable weather, there's no better way than camping to see natural beauty and wildlife up close.

   a. Camping trips are rarely affected by rain or other problems.

   b. Camping trips are sometimes affected by rain or other problems.

FROM READING TO WRITING

Reflecting on the Reading

Discuss the questions in pairs or small groups.

Journal
Choose one question and write a journal entry.

1. What is the most enjoyable vacation that you have ever taken? What made it enjoyable? Did planning help to make it a good trip?
2. Imagine you are taking a vacation. How will the following factors influence your planning: time, money, and natural features or activities at the place? Explain.
3. Which of these features of a vacation do you consider the most important? Rank them from 1 (the most important) to 5 (the least important).
   My vacation should be . . .
   _____ safe
   _____ relaxing
   _____ fast-paced
   _____ educational
   _____ amusing

Activating Your Vocabulary

Think about the sport or leisure activity you wrote about in Chapter 7. Take notes on these questions. Try to use your answers in your Writing Assignment.

Vocabulary
For more practice with vocabulary, go to page 199.

1. What are the **economic** factors in playing that sport or doing that activity?
2. Is a lot of planning necessary **ahead of time**?
3. Is this a solo sport or activity or does it involve competitors or **companions**?
4. Does this sport or activity take place at a particular **site**? What types of **facilities** does it require?
5. What plans for supplies or schedules do you need to **arrange** in advance?

Writing the Body and Conclusion of a Process Essay

Remember that a process essay tells how to do something or how something works. The introductory paragraph contains the thesis statement and tells how you will present the process. (See page 76 for more about writing an introduction.) The rest of the essay consists of the **body paragraphs** and the **concluding paragraph**.

Body Paragraphs

The body of a process essay should explain the steps of the process. Typically, the first body paragraph includes:

- materials needed to complete the process
- the result or purpose of the process
- the beginning steps of the process

Divide the steps of the process into logical groups, with each group being one paragraph. The steps should be explained clearly and completely and include warnings or tips to help readers. Begin each body paragraph with a topic sentence and include appropriate supporting details.

Conclusion

An effective conclusion brings an essay to a close by restating the thesis or summarizing main points made in the essay. Add interest to the conclusion by including a result, a prediction, a recommendation, or a quotation.

These questions will help you choose an appropriate conclusion style:

- **Result** What will happen at the end of the process?
- **Prediction** What will happen in the future? When will it happen?
- **Recommendation** What do you recommend or suggest? How can this happen?
- **Quotation** Is there an interesting quotation that emphasizes the main idea or raises a final point?

Reread the conclusion from "Playing Sudoku" shown below. Notice that the final sentence makes a prediction.

> Sudoku is not the ideal leisure-time activity for everyone, but if you like a mental challenge, try it. You might agree with sudoku lovers that this little puzzle is making the world smarter.

Practice

A. *Read the introduction and conclusion of this essay. Identify the writer's conclusion style: result, prediction, recommendation, or quotation.*

A Dream Come True

Introduction My friend Christian Rodriguez always dreamed of having his own business. At times, he didn't think he would reach his goal, but eventually he succeeded. He worked his way through high school and college, and now, at age 25, he owns a property management business. By studying, working hard, and saving money, Christian was able to achieve his dream.

. . .

Conclusion Now with a successful business, Christian no longer needs to study, work so hard, or watch his money so closely, but he still does. He serves as a role model for his younger relatives and friends, urging them to attend to school, work, and save money. "I always knew I could do it," Christian tells them. "I know you can do it, too."

B. *Answer the following questions about "A Dream Come True."*

1. Which sentence is the thesis statement? Underline it.

2. How many body paragraphs do you expect this essay to have? _____

3. What ideas will you find in the body paragraphs? List them.

   _____

   _____

   _____

4. Which two conclusion styles did the writer combine in the conclusion?

   _____

C. *Work in pairs. Write a new conclusion for the essay, using a different style.*

   _____

   _____

   _____

   _____

   _____

WRITING ASSIGNMENT

Write a process essay using the introductory paragraph that you wrote in Chapter 7. Follow the steps.

STEP 1 **Get ideas.**

A. Review your topic choice and your introduction. Make changes if necessary.

❑ **Topic 1:** How to play a sport or game

❑ **Topic 2:** How to do a leisure-time activity

B. List the steps of the process.

EXAMPLE

Steps for Planning a Camping Trip

Borrow or buy the basic camping equipment you will need: tents,

blankets, pillows, cooking utensils, and flashlights.

Make a list of the meals you plan to prepare.

List the ingredients and cooking equipment you will need.

C. Work in groups. Read your introductory paragraph and steps. Discuss if you have missed any steps.

D. You should repeat key ideas from your introduction in the conclusion. List key words or phrases you will use.

STEP 2 **Organize your ideas.**

Organize the body paragraphs into logical paragraph groups. Choose an appropriate conclusion style. Use the writing skill information on page 86. Show your ideas to your instructor before you write.

STEP 3 **Write a rough draft.**

Write your essay. Use your information from Steps 1 and 2. Include vocabulary from the chapter where possible.

STEP 4 Revise your rough draft.

Read your essay. Use the Writing Checklist to look for mistakes. Work alone or in pairs.

> ### Writing Checklist
> ❑ Does your introduction present the process and catch the reader's interest?
> ❑ Does each body paragraph explain a step or a group of steps in the process?
> ❑ Is the whole process logical and complete?
> ❑ Did you include tips and warnings for the readers?
> ❑ Did your conclusion restate the thesis statement and use an appropriate conclusion style?
> ❑ Did you use vocabulary from the chapter appropriately?

STEP 5 Edit your writing.

A. Edit your essay. Correct any mistakes in capitalization, punctuation, spelling, or verb use.

B. Exchange essays with a partner. Use the Correction Symbols on page 201 to mark each other's work.

EXAMPLE

PUNCTUATION ERROR (P)

, for

I enjoy many sports in my free time. For example, basketball and soccer.

STEP 6 Write a final copy.

Correct your mistakes. Copy your final essay and give it to your instructor.

UNIT FIVE

Relationships

Six Degrees of Separation

PRE-READING

Discussion

Discuss the questions in pairs or small groups.

1. Look at the photographs. Can you explain how these people might be connected with each other in some way? For example, could they be neighbors, teachers, co-workers, or friends?
2. The reading in this chapter says that everybody in the world could be connected to one another. Do you believe that is possible? Explain.

Vocabulary

Read the sentences. Match the boldfaced words with the definitions.

__*g*__ 1. There is a **theory** that all humans came from Africa. Scientists have evidence to suggest that this is true.

_____ 2. How is studying **linked to** doing well on tests? Does one affect the other?

_____ 3. Several times I told my classmate to call me, but he never did. Should I **assume** that he is not interested in being my friend?

_____ 4. If you have **contact** with someone who has the flu, you may get sick, too. Be careful of spending too much time with people who can pass their sickness to you.

_____ 5. Sometimes I **am aware of** my bad habits. For example, I realize when I am talking too much.

_____ 6. Anders has **roughly** 50 people in his family. This number is not exact, but it's about the total of his parents, siblings, aunts and uncles, cousins, and grandparents.

_____ 7. What is the **extent** of your travels? Have you traveled a lot or only a little?

_____ 8. An interesting **chain** of events caused me to meet my boyfriend. By chance, he sat next to me in a class, and then we became friends.

_____ 9. Mr. Jones and his classmates have **mutual** respect. He respects them, and they respect him.

---

a. range or scope of something
b. shared by two or more people
c. connected to
d. a set of connected things
e. believe that something is true without proof
f. realize that something is true, exists, or is happening
g. an explanation for something that may be reasonable, but has not yet been proven to be true
h. not exactly; about
i. the state of touching or being close to someone or something

---

Six Degrees of Separation

1   You've probably heard the phrase *six degrees of separation*. There's a movie and a play with the same name. But the idea behind the name is much more fascinating than the shows themselves. The name refers to the **theory** of six degrees of separation. This theory says that all people on earth are **linked to** each other in some way. For example, you may not know my second cousin Omar, but if you look carefully, you may, or rather *will*, find a link between you and him. The link could be a **mutual** friend or an old classmate, or someone you did business with at some point in your life, who knew someone else who had known someone, and so forth. Everyone can link him or herself with everyone else in the world with no more than six people in between.

2   Actually, when you think about it, you can appreciate the **extent** to which this is amazing. Consider that there are **roughly** seven billion people on earth. How long would it take you to count them all? You might guess that it would take several days or weeks. Guess again, use a calculator, and you will realize that it would take you several hundred years if you spent day and night just counting. Shaking everyone's hand on this earth, **assuming** they were lined up and it took you only one second for each person, would take 1,000 years as a full-time occupation, with a couple of weeks of vacation a year. If you also stopped to exchange a greeting with each person, that might take five or ten thousand years.

3   Now, to go back to the theory. Let me take an example from my own life. While I was discussing this subject with a Chinese friend more than 30 years ago, he asked what the link might be between me and Mao Zedong, the former head of state of China. I thought for a few seconds. Then I asked *him* if he had ever needed to speak with his consul[1] in the United States. He said that he had. I told my friend that was the link: I knew him, and he shook the consul's hand. The consul obviously had to shake hands (or greet in some way) the ambassador,[2] who is his superior. The ambassador, in turn,[3] must have had **contact** with the then Chinese head of state since he was appointed[4] by him. That is only *three* degrees of separation, and this is one link that I **am aware of**. There may very well be shorter connections that I am simply unaware of.

4   Using famous people or public officials as examples may be cheating, though. These persons are at the crossroads[5] between many people. However, there are many other people in other positions, such as doctors, teachers, store employees, police and other law enforcement officers, government employees, and so on, whom everyone of us is sure to deal with at some point in our lives. Consider that many of these people belong to organizations or professional associations and

---

[1] **consul:** an official who lives in a foreign city and whose job is to help citizens of his/her own country who also live or work there
[2] **ambassador:** an important official who represents his/her country in another country
[3] **in turn:** in proper order or sequence
[4] **appoint:** to choose someone for a job, position, etc.
[5] **crossroads:** a point where a choice must be made

go to meetings every year. For example, if you go to the doctor once in a while, that doctor has probably attended many professional conventions. So, too, it's likely that your teacher goes to conventions and speaks to teachers from all over the world. The same goes for other professions as well. Professionals that we meet come into contact with other professionals at conferences and meetings. In this way, human **chains** of contacts exist that we are not aware of.

5   The theory remains true on a wider scale, too. Today, we live in an electronic age. Researchers have tested the six degrees theory using e-mail. Columbia University professor Duncan Watt and his research team sent e-mail messages to 19 target people in 157 countries. Watt had to get the messages to his targets by electronic contacts with humans, not with Google[6] searches. As in a similar study in 1967, Watt found that the average number of people in between was six.[7]

6   It's amazing that the world we live in is so connected. Seven billion people are spread out over all the continents[8] and separated by oceans and seas. Yet we are all truly linked. If each one of us carried disease, we would all become ill. If each of us had some kind of healing power, we would all be healthy. When you think of your own life—and the connections that you have with everyone around you—you can realize how small the world really is.

[6] **Google™:** Google, a popular search engine, is a tool for finding resources on the Internet.
[7] **Duncan Watt:** See http://smallworld.columbia.edu/watts.html for bibliography of Watt's publications.
[8] **continent:** one of the main areas of land on the earth

Identifying Main Ideas

Which paragraphs discuss these main ideas? Write the number of the paragraph.

_____ **a.** Human chains of contacts happen between people that they may not be aware of.

_____ **b.** All people on earth are linked in some way.

_____ **c.** Even in electronic communication, there are usually six people connecting any two people.

_____ **d.** The six degrees of separation theory is amazing because of the number of people on the earth.

_____ **e.** There are only three degrees of separation between the author and Mao Zedong.

Identifying Details

Match the people with the descriptions.

_____ 1. Common friends or old classmates

_____ 2. Doctors and teachers

_____ 3. Famous people

_____ 4. University researchers

a. are at the crossroads between many people.

b. have tested the six degrees theory in an e-mail study.

c. may link you with someone that you do not know.

d. attend conferences where they meet people.

Making Inferences

What meaning can be inferred from the passage? Circle the letter of the best answer.

1. It's a theory called six degrees of separation. It says that all people on earth are linked in some way to each other. That is, you may not know my second cousin Omar, but if you look carefully, you may, or rather *will*, find a link between you and him.

   a. The writer believes that the idea of six degrees of separation is only a theory, not a proven fact.

   b. The writer believes that the idea of six degrees of separation is more than a theory; it is likely true.

2. If each one of us carried disease, we would all become ill. If each of us had some kind of healing power, we would all be healthy.

   a. The writer wants to say that people are very connected.

   b. The writer wants to say that people face many health risks.

READING SKILL

Recognizing Cohesive Devices

Cohesive devices are words that link ideas in a reading. They help you understand relationships among ideas in a text. Writers use cohesive devices to emphasize what is important and to add cohesion, or unity, to their writing.

Here are three common types of cohesive devices:

- **Pronouns and antecedents**

    EXAMPLE

    I made a new **friend** yesterday. **He** is in my English class.

    An **antecedent** is the word to which a pronoun refers. In this example, the pronoun *he* refers to the antecedent *friend*. The **pronoun** *he* is a cohesive device.

- **Repeated words**

    EXAMPLE

    Maddy's new **car** is a red Honda Civic. It gets good gas mileage. She really loves her **car.**

    Here, the word *car* in the third sentence is a cohesive device. It repeats the idea of car from the first sentence. (The pronoun *it* in the second sentence also refers to *car* in the first sentence.)

- **Synonyms for earlier stated words**

    EXAMPLE

    The six degrees of separation **theory** is fascinating. Since I read the article, I've been thinking about the **idea** a great deal.

    In this example, the word *idea* is a cohesive device. It is a synonym for *theory* in the first sentence.

Practice

Read each passage below. Circle the cohesive devices in each passage. Draw arrows from each cohesive device to the word(s) that it refers to. The first one is done for you. Compare your answers in pairs or small groups.

1. *Six degrees of separation* is a fascinating theory, but where did it all start?

2. A Hungarian writer named Frigyes Karinthy came up with the six degrees theory in 1929. He introduced his idea about the links among people on earth in a short story called "Chains."

3. In 1967, sociologist Stanley Milgram renamed Frigyes Karinthy's theory "the small world problem." Milgram tested the idea by asking people in the United States to send packages to people they did not know.

4. In Milgram's study, each sender received one person's name, occupation, and the general area where the person lived. Each sender had to mail the package to someone he or she knew. The goal was to get the package to the target person. Surprisingly, it took on average five to seven people in between to get each package to its target.

FROM READING TO WRITING

Journal
Choose one question and write a journal entry.

Reflecting on the Reading

Discuss the questions in pairs or small groups.

1. Do you have a friend that you met through another person? Describe the way that you met this friend.
2. Do you know someone who has a lot of friends? How does this person make friends easily?
3. Do you feel that you have a connection to a famous person that you have not met? If so, is that connection important to you?

Vocabulary
For more practice with vocabulary, go to page 200.

Activating Your Vocabulary

Take notes on these questions. Try to use your answers in your Writing Assignment.

1. Do you and one of your friends have a **mutual** acquaintance? Who is the person?
2. Are you **linked to** any famous people?
3. Do you believe the **theory** of six degrees of separation?
4. What is the **extent** of your friendships? Do you make **contact** with others easily or with more difficulty?
5. Are you **aware of** any connections to people in other countries?

Writing a Summary

A **summary** states the main idea and major supporting points of a reading. The summary should be much shorter than the original text. Here are the steps for writing a summary:

- **Read the original text twice.** Read once for main ideas and again to make sure that you understand. Highlight or underline the main ideas and major supporting points. Study the underlining in this paragraph from "Six Degrees of Separation."

  EXAMPLE

  You've probably heard the phrase _six degrees of separation_. There's a movie and a play with the same name. But the idea behind the name is much more fascinating than the shows themselves. The name refers to <u>the theory of six degrees of separation. This theory says that all people on earth are linked in some way to each other.</u> For example, you may not know my second cousin Omar, but if you look carefully, you may, or rather _will,_ find a link between you and him. The link could be a mutual friend or an old classmate, or someone you did business with at some point in your life, who knew someone else who had known someone, and so forth. <u>Everyone can link him or herself with everyone else in the world with no more than six people in between.</u>

- **Take notes and organize your ideas.** Make a list of the major points of the reading.

Summary of "Six Degrees of Separation"

– all the people in the world: connected with six or fewer

    people between

– thousands of years to greet everyone on earth

– example: the writer's connection to Mao Zedong through a friend

– professionals: give us connections with others that we don't

    know about

– Columbia U. e-mail study, six degrees of separation theory tested

– entire world: connected

- **Follow an introduction-body-conclusion format.** Start your summary with a sentence that states the title of the reading, the author (if known), and the main idea of the reading.

  EXAMPLE

  > The article "Six Degrees of Separation" explains the theory that everyone in the world is linked to each other.

- **Keep it brief.** Write *one or two sentences* about each major point in the body. Do not include specific details.
- **Use your own words.** Restate the writer's ideas, but do not change the writer's meaning. Give the writer credit for ideas, with phrases such as "the writer says" or "according to the article."
- **Do not include your opinions.**
- **Conclude with a sentence that restates the writer's main idea.**

Practice

Match each summary with one of the descriptions on the next page. Write the letter of the description in the box. Then discuss your answers in pairs or small groups.

Paragraph 1

☐

In "Six Degrees of Separation," the author presents the theory that the world is really a small place. The Internet connects everyone because it is easy to communicate through e-mail and computers. The author also believes that it would take 1,000 years for us to greet everyone on earth, but with today's technology, this doesn't seem true. I can't take the article seriously because of this. It doesn't seem possible that everyone in the world is connected.

Paragraph 2

☐

In this article, the author talks about separation between people. The writer is connected to the former Chinese leader, Mao Zedong. About 30 years ago, the writer knew a Chinese friend in the United States. The writer's friend had a problem, so he had to see his consul. The consul shook his hand. The writer's friend was, therefore, connected to the consul's boss—the ambassador to the United States. The ambassador was most likely connected to Mao Zedong. All of these connections show how the writer was connected to Mao Zedong.

Paragraph 3

☐

In "Six Degrees of Separation," the author explains the theory that everyone on earth is connected. Every person is connected by no more than six people, even though it would take a thousand years for someone to greet all the people on earth. The author uses the example of his own connection to the Chinese leader Mao Zedong through a Chinese friend in the United States. Furthermore, the writer says that we are connected to others in ways that we don't know about. This happens because we meet professionals such as doctors who go to conferences and meet many other people. Recent research at Columbia University showed that the theory is true. According to the writer, the people of the world are truly connected.

Descriptions of Summaries

a. This summary states the title, but it does not state the main idea of the article accurately. This summary gives new information that the author did not write about. The summary should not include personal opinions. This is not a good summary.

b. This summary begins with a sentence that states the title and accurately states the main idea of the article. It focuses on the main idea, includes the one main example presented in the reading, and includes the writer's other major points. This is a good summary.

c. This summary does not include the name of the article. It also states the article's main idea inaccurately. This summary gives too many specific details. It does not focus on the major points of the reading. This is not a good summary.

WRITING ASSIGNMENT

Write a one-paragraph summary of the article below, "The Queen and I." Follow the steps.

STEP 1   Get ideas.

Read the article. Read first for main ideas. Then read again for better understanding. As you read, highlight or underline the main idea and major supporting points.

The Queen and I

I'm an average college student living in the United States—not a king or queen but, amazingly, I have a connection with Queen Elizabeth II of Great Britain. My mother had an experience more than 25 years ago that links me to the queen.

Naturally, I know my mother. Years ago, my mother was a journalist. In her work, she met many famous people. In 1980, in Houston, Texas, she had an assignment to report on the visit of Great Britain's Princess Margaret to the United States. My mother met the princess in a reception at the British consulate in Houston. At the reception, she stood in line to shake hands with

Princess Margaret and exchange words with her. She describes the princess as beautiful and charming, and remembers welcoming her to the United States. It was a brief exchange, but they did meet.

As Queen Elizabeth II's younger sister, of course, Princess Margaret knew her sister all of her life. Queen Elizabeth was born in 1926, and Margaret was born in 1930 and died in 2002. The two sisters were the only children of their parents, so they were undoubtedly close. They were educated together and lived together until Elizabeth married.

It's interesting to think that I can connect myself with a queen even though I've never met her. Moreover, Queen Elizabeth II has had contact with many other important people in her lifetime, so my connections go well beyond her. Who knows how many other kings, queens, or presidents of countries that I have connections with?

STEP 2   **Organize your ideas.**

A. Make a list of the main idea and major points in the reading. Work in pairs and compare your lists.

B. Write a sentence that states the title, author, and main idea of the reading. Show your sentence to your instructor.

C. Organize your summary in the introduction-body-conclusion format. Use the steps from the writing skill on page 99.

STEP 3   **Write a rough draft.**

Write your summary. Include vocabulary from the chapter where possible.

STEP 4   **Revise your rough draft.**

Read your paragraph. Use the Writing Checklist to look for mistakes. Work alone or in pairs.

Writing Checklist

❑ Does your summary begin with a sentence that states the title, author, and main idea?

❑ Did you follow the introduction-body-conclusion format?

❑ Did you use your own words?

❑ Did you avoid including your opinions?

❑ Did you use repetition and restatement to emphasize main ideas and unify your writing?

❑ Did you use vocabulary from the chapter appropriately?

STEP 5   **Edit your writing.**

   A. Edit your summary. Correct any mistakes in capitalization, punctuation, spelling, or verb use.

   B. Exchange summaries with a partner. Use the Correction Symbols on page 191 to mark each other's work.

   EXAMPLE

WORD FORM ERROR (**wf**)

connection

Gina and I have a strong ~~connect~~ because we attended the same high school.

STEP 6   **Write a final copy.**

Correct your mistakes. Copy your final summary and give it to your instructor.

Table for Two

*In this chapter
you will:*

• read a story
about how a
couple met

• learn how to
state and
support an
opinion about a
reading

• write a response
to a reading

A table for two

PRE-READING

Discussion

Discuss the questions in pairs or small groups.

1. Study the photograph. How would you describe the relationship between the two people?
2. Tell the story of how you met an important person in your life. How and where did you meet? What was your first impression of this person?
3. Is it possible to fall in love when you first meet someone? Explain.

Vocabulary

Circle the letter of the word or phrase that is closest in meaning to the boldfaced word.

1. Melissa is a busy student who studies and takes classes **throughout** the day.

   a. during all   b. after   c. every

2. If you **are willing to** meet at 5:00 P.M. every Monday and Thursday, you can join our study group.

   a. want to   b. need to   c. are ready to

3. I **barely** finished reading the biology chapter before it was time for class.

   a. didn't finish   b. just finished   c. almost finished

4. My classmates and I were **entirely** interested in the professor's topic, so we listened closely.

   a. completely   b. finally   c. strongly

5. If you're hungry, let's try that new sandwich shop at the **edge** of town.

   a. center   b. part   c. end

6. The library was **deserted** earlier this morning, but now it's crowded.

   a. full   b. empty   c. occupied

7. If you have **neglected** to call your friends recently, they may forget you!

   a. remembered   b. forgotten   c. hoped

8. **Apparently**, this pizza place isn't very good. I rarely see any customers there.

   a. actually   b. it seems like   c. surprisingly

9. My friends and I were **determined** to buy all our school clothes in one day, so we shopped from morning to evening!

   a. uncertain   b. persistently set   c. helped

10. I was trying to concentrate on my reading, but the telephone **interrupted** me.

    a. stopped   b. frightened   c. concerned

Table for Two

By Lori Peikoff

1   In 1947 my mother, Deborah, was a 21-year-old student at New York University, majoring in English literature. She was beautiful—fiery, yet introspective[1]—with a great passion for books and ideas. She read all the time and hoped one day to become a writer.

2   My father, Joseph, was an aspiring[2] painter who supported himself by teaching art at a junior high school on the West Side. On Saturdays, he would paint all day, either at home or in Central Park, and treat himself to a meal out. On the Saturday night in question, he chose a neighborhood restaurant called Milky Way.

3   The Milky Way happened to be my mother's favorite restaurant, and that Saturday, after studying **throughout** the morning and afternoon, she went there for dinner, carrying along a used copy of Dickens's *Great Expectations*.[3] The restaurant was crowded, and she was given the last table. She settled in for an evening of goulash,[4] red wine, and Dickens—and quickly **lost track of**[5] what was going on around her.

4   Within half an hour, the restaurant was standing-room-only. The frazzled[6] hostess came over and asked my mother if she would **be willing to** share her table with someone else. **Barely** glancing up from her book, my mother agreed.

5   Joseph approached the table, and when he saw the tattered[7] cover of *Great Expectations*, he said, "A tragic life for poor dear Pip." My mother looked up at him, and at that moment, she recalls, she saw something strangely familiar in his eyes. Years later, when I begged her to tell me the story one more time, she sighed sweetly and said, "I saw myself in his eyes."

6   My father, **entirely** captivated[8] by the presence before him, swears to this day that he heard a voice inside his head. "She is your destiny,"[9] the voice said, and immediately after that he felt a tingling sensation that ran from the tip of his toes to the crown of his head. Whatever it was that my parents saw or heard or felt that night, they both understood that something miraculous had happened.

7   Like two old friends catching up after a long absence from one another, they talked for hours. Later on, when the evening was over, Deborah wrote her phone number on the inside cover of *Great Expectations* and gave the book to my father. He said good-bye to her, gently kissing her on the forehead,

---

[1]**introspective:** thinking deeply about your own thoughts and feelings
[2]**aspiring:** An aspiring painter is someone who is trying to become a painter.
[3]**Dickens:** Charles Dickens (1812-1870), English author of *Great Expectations* (1861), a novel about an orphan's life
[4]**goulash:** a dish made of meat cooked in liquid with a hot tasting pepper
[5]**lost track of:** failed to pay attention to something so that you know where it is or what is happening

[6]**frazzled:** confused, tired, and worried
[7]**tattered:** old and torn
[8]**captivated:** attracted and interested
[9]**destiny:** the things that will happen in the future, or the power that controls what happens

and then they walked off in opposite directions into the night.

8   Neither one of them was able to sleep. Even after she closed her eyes, my mother could only see one thing: my father's face. And my father, who could not stop thinking about her, stayed up all night painting my mother's portrait.

9   The next day, Sunday, he traveled out to Brooklyn to visit his parents. He brought along the book to read on the subway, but he was exhausted after his sleepless night and started feeling drowsy after just a few paragraphs. So he slipped the book into the pocket of his coat—which he had put on the seat next to him—and closed his eyes. He didn't wake up until the train stopped at Brighton Beach, at the far **edge** of Brooklyn.

10   The train was **deserted** by then, and when he opened his eyes, the coat was no longer there. Someone had stolen it, and because the book was in the pocket, the book was gone, too. Which meant that my mother's telephone number was also gone. In desperation,[10] he began to search the train, looking under every seat, not only in his car but in the cars on either side of him. In his excitement over meeting Deborah the night before, he had foolishly **neglected** to find out her last name. The telephone number was his only link to her.

11   The call that my mother was expecting never came. My father went looking for her several times at the NYU English Department, he could never find her. Destiny had betrayed[11] them both. What had seemed inevitable[12] that first night in the restaurant was **apparently** not meant to be.

12   That summer, they both headed for Europe. My mother went to England to take literature courses at Oxford, and my father went to Paris to paint. In late July, with a three-day break in her studies, my mother flew to Paris, **determined** to absorb as much culture as she possibly could in 72 hours. She carried along a new copy of *Great Expectations* on the trip. After the sad business with my father, she hadn't had the heart to read it, but now, as she sat down in a crowded restaurant after a long day of sight-seeing, she opened it to the first page and started thinking about him again.

13   After reading a few sentences, she was **interrupted** by the maitre d'[13] who asked her, first in French, then in broken English, if she wouldn't mind sharing her table. She agreed and then returned to her reading. A moment later, she heard a familiar voice.

14   "A tragic life for poor dear Pip," the voice said, and then she looked up, and there he was again.

---

[10] **desperation:** a strong feeling that you will do anything to change a very bad situation

[11] **betray:** harm or be disloyal
[12] **inevitable:** certain to happen and impossible to avoid
[13] **maitre d':** the host or head waiter at a restaurant

Identifying Main Ideas

Read each question. Circle the letter of the best answer.

1. What is the writer's main point in the article?
   a. She describes her parents when they were young.
   b. She explains her mother's love of reading.
   c. She describes how her father lost her mother's book.
   d. She tells the story of how her mother and father met.

2. In paragraphs 5–7, how does the writer describe her parents' meeting?
   a. They did not believe in miracles.
   b. They had an immediate attraction to each other.
   c. They had known each other before this evening.
   d. They did not react strongly to each other.

3. In paragraphs 9 and 10, what happened on the train?
   a. The man couldn't sleep.
   b. The man read a book.
   c. The man fell asleep.
   d. The train was crowded.

Identifying Details

Which main character, Deborah or Joseph, do these phrases describe? Mark them D (Deborah) or J (Joseph).

_____ 1. hoped to be a painter

_____ 2. hoped to be a writer

_____ 3. read all the time

_____ 4. said, "A tragic life for poor dear Pip."

_____ 5. studied at New York University

_____ 6. taught at a junior high school

_____ 7. wanted to share a table

_____ 8. visited parents by train

_____ 9. was sitting alone at a table

_____ 10. went to Europe to study

Making Inferences

What meaning can be inferred from the passage? Circle the letter of the best answer.

1. He approached the table, and when he saw the tattered cover of *Great Expectations,* he said, "A tragic life for poor dear Pip."

   a. The man knew the book well enough to remember the first line.

   b. The man remembered someone named Pip when he saw the book.

2. She carried along a new copy of *Great Expectations* on the trip. After the sad business with my father, she hadn't had the heart to read it.

   a. The woman did not want to read the book because she was angry at the man.

   b. The woman did not want to read the book because she was disappointed that she had not seen the man again.

3. A moment later, she heard a familiar voice. "A tragic life for poor dear Pip," the voice said, and then she looked up, and there he was again.

   a. The writer wants to show that this was a surprising event.

   b. The writer wants to show that this was a sad event.

FROM READING TO WRITING

Journal
Choose one question and write a journal entry.

Reflecting on the Reading

Discuss the questions in pairs or small groups.

1. Read paragraphs 5 and 6 of the reading again. How would you describe the way the couple reacted to each other? Do you think this kind of reaction really happens?
2. Read paragraphs 13 and 14 of the reading again. Do you think this kind of situation happens often? Do you believe the writer's story?
3. Can you think of a time when you met someone and had an immediate positive or negative reaction to him or her? Explain what happened.

Vocabulary
For more practice with vocabulary, go to page 201.

Activating Your Vocabulary

Take notes on these questions. Try to use your answers in your Writing Assignment.

1. Deborah was **determined** to learn as much as she could. What have you ever been determined to do or accomplish?
2. Joseph had **neglected** to get Deborah's last name. Have you ever neglected to find out something and later regretted it?

3. Joseph was **entirely** captivated by Deborah. Have you ever had that feeling?

4. Have you ever been **willing to** share a table, taxi, or room with another? Was your outcome similar to or different from the story?

5. Deborah and Joseph thought about each other **throughout** the months between their meetings. Have you ever thought about someone for a long time? How did you feel during that time?

WRITING

**WRITING
SKILL**

Writing a Response to a Reading

A **response** to a reading is different from a summary of a reading. A response should include your opinions. Often in a response, you answer a question or questions about the main idea of the reading.

Steps for Writing a Response

1. Read the assigned text for main ideas, and then reread it for better understanding. As you read, mark main ideas, major supporting points, and interesting ideas.

2. Read the question(s) or topic(s) of your assignment. Here are some common types of response assignments:
   - *Agree or disagree* with a main idea in the reading.
   - *Compare* and/or *contrast* what you read with your experiences.
   - *Evaluate* a main idea in the reading.

   EXAMPLE

   > Do you agree or disagree with the theory presented in "Six Degrees of Separation"? Explain your reasons.

3. Begin your response with one sentence that gives the title and author of the reading (if given) and states your opinion (the answer to the assigned topic or question).

   EXAMPLE

   > The article "Six Degrees of Separation" states that everyone in the world is connected, but I disagree with this theory.

4. Follow the introduction-body-conclusion format. In the body of your essay, focus on answering the topic question in more detail. Support your opinion with reasons, using ideas from the reading and your own ideas.

5. Use phrases to identify the writer's ideas and your ideas.

EXAMPLE

┌──────── THE WRITER'S IDEAS ────────┐

"The author states that . . ." or "In the article, . . ."

┌──────── YOUR IDEAS ────────┐

"I agree with this because . . ." or "However, I believe that . . ."

6. Close with a conclusion that restates your opinion (the idea in your first sentence).

Practice

A. *Read the article. Then read the response topic and the model response which follow the article.*

A Chance Meeting

You never know where you will meet someone who knows someone that you know. It could be on a train, in a restaurant, or on the street. A shopping trip led me to a man who had met my uncle halfway across the world before I was born.

I was a university student when I went shopping one day with my friends in New York City. It was 1979, and I had just arrived in the United States. My friends and I happened to walk into a clothing store owned by a friendly Mexican-American. The shop owner and I started talking, and he asked me where I was from. I told him that I was from Algeria, and as it often happens, he said he knew some Algerians. I did not think that we would actually have common acquaintances, but I listened to his story.

In fact, the man had served in the U.S. Army during World War II and had traveled to Algeria in 1944. He said he had frequently eaten at one particular café in Algiers, the capital city. When he mentioned the name, I recognized it instantly. It was a café called The Sphinx where I thought one of my uncles had once worked. After I got home from the man's store, I called my uncle. Indeed, he had worked at the café as a waiter in 1944. He said that without a doubt, if the man was a regular customer there, then he had served him.

This encounter shows that you never know when you will meet someone who is linked to you in some way. In this case, the chain of contacts was surprising because it crossed time and space, from before my birth to a completely different part of the world.

Response Topic

Evaluate this statement from "A Chance Meeting": "In this case, the chain of contacts was surprising because it crossed time and space, from before my birth to a completely different part of the world." Do you agree that the writer's experience was very uncommon and surprising? Or do you think it was something that commonly happens to people?

Model Response

The writer of "A Chance Meeting" says that his experience was surprising, and I agree. First of all, it's uncommon to meet somebody who knows one of your friends or family members from a different country. According to the article, the writer was in New York City, and his family lives in Algeria. Even more surprising was learning that a person in New York knew the writer's uncle—before the writer was even born. When you think of someone in the U.S. Army going to a café in Africa, you wonder how that person could be connected to an African in New York. However, the writer said that the minute he heard the name of the café, he recognized the connection. The writer thought it was a surprising meeting. I agree because I've never heard of that happening to anyone I know. I believe the writer's story is very rare and surprising.

B. Follow the instructions. Then work in small groups and compare your answers.

1. What type of response topic was assigned? Circle the letter of the answer.

   a. agree or disagree **b.** compare and/ or contrast **c.** evaluate

2. Circle these phrases in the model response.
   "According to the article"   "I agree"   "I believe"

3. Underline sentences where the writer supports his or her opinion with ideas from the reading and his or her own ideas.

WRITING ASSIGNMENT

Write a one-paragraph response to "Table for Two." Follow the steps.

STEP 1   **Get ideas.**

A. Read "Table for Two" again.

B. Choose a topic for your response. Check (✔) it.

❑ **Topic 1:**   In "Table for Two," Deborah waited for a telephone call that "never came." Compare and/or contrast the woman's situation with one that happened to you. Did you ever wait for a call from someone? Was the ending of your story similar to or different from Deborah's?

❑ **Topic 2:**   At the end of "Table for Two," we learn that Deborah did not want to read *Great Expectations* before she came to Europe because of the "sad business" with Joseph. Do you agree that this was a "sad business"? Did Deborah have a good reason to feel sad? Explain.

C. Write the first sentence of your response. Be sure to include your opinion.

EXAMPLE

Topic 1:   I had a situation similar to Deborah's but my situation ended differently.

Topic 2:   In the story "Table for Two," Deborah has a good reason to feel sad.

STEP 2   **Organize your ideas.**

Follow this format to organize your one-paragraph response.

• **Introduction:** State your opinion (the answer to the topic questions) in your first sentence.
• **Body sentences:** Support your opinion with reasons. Use ideas from the reading and your own ideas to explain your reasons. Use phrases to identify the writer's ideas and your ideas.
• **Conclusion sentence:** Conclude by restating your opinion.

STEP 3   **Write a rough draft.**

Write your response. Use the format from Step 2. Include vocabulary from the chapter where possible.

STEP 4   Revise your rough draft.

Read your response and look for mistakes. Use the Writing Checklist.
Work alone or in pairs.

Writing Checklist

❑ Does your response begin with a sentence that states your opinion
(the answer to the topic question)?

❑ Did you follow the introduction-body-conclusion format?

❑ Did you use your own words?

❑ Did you give reasons to support your opinion?

❑ Did you support the reasons with ideas from the reading and your
ideas?

❑ Did you use phrases to identify the writer's ideas and your own
ideas?

❑ Did you use vocabulary from the chapter appropriately?

STEP 5   Edit your writing.

A. Edit your response. Correct any mistakes in capitalization,
punctuation, spelling, or verb use.

B. Exchange responses with a partner. Use the Correction Symbols on
page 191 to mark each other's work.

EXAMPLE

WORD FORM ERROR (wf)

My neighborhood introduced me to the girl who later became my
girlfriend.

STEP 6   Write a final copy.

Correct your mistakes. Copy your final response and give it to your
instructor.

UNIT SIX

Money Matters

Generation Broke

**In this chapter
you will:**

- read an article
about young
people and debt

- learn strategies
for identifying
cause and effect

- organize and
write a proposal
for a cause-effect
essay

Student debt

PRE-READING

Discussion

Discuss the questions in pairs or small groups.

1. Look at the drawing. What does it say about young people and debt (money that you owe to someone)?
2. The title of the chapter is "Generation Broke." *Broke* means "having no money." Which generation do you think is the most broke? Explain.
3. Do you know someone who is *deep in debt,* in other words, someone who has a lot of debt? If so, explain the situation.

Vocabulary

Circle the letter of the word or phrase that is NOT close in meaning to the boldfaced word.

1. Technology plays a greater role in life for my **generation** than it did for my parents' generation.
   - **a.** age group
   - **b.** time period
   - **c.** family *(circled)*

2. My friend Jenny faced a money **crisis** when she lost her job, but luckily, her parents helped her out.
   - **a.** major problem
   - **b.** disaster
   - **c.** achievement

3. Tarsha has so many bills that she thinks about them all the time. Her bills are like a heavy **load** on her mind.
   - **a.** burden
   - **b.** charge
   - **c.** weight

4. Paulo is **struggling** to pay all his bills. He tries to cut costs, but he doesn't end up with enough money at the end of the month.
   - **a.** pushing back
   - **b.** trying hard
   - **c.** working hard

5. Today, we use computers in nearly every part of our lives. People in **previous** generations did not have computers.
   - **a.** earlier
   - **b.** past
   - **c.** new

6. For one week, Jim kept records of his spending. After an **analysis** of the records, he found that food was his greatest expense.
   - **a.** study
   - **b.** investigation
   - **c.** result

7. Todd wants to **pursue** a higher degree, but he cannot because he still needs to pay back loans for his first college degree.
   - **a.** follow
   - **b.** organize
   - **c.** work to achieve

8. **Anxiety** is a typical result of money problems. When people don't have money, they get nervous about their future.
   - **a.** doubt
   - **b.** hope
   - **c.** worry

9. If you want to **get ahead** financially, you must learn to save money.
   - **a.** advance
   - **b.** be successful
   - **c.** better understand

10. Martina uses her credit card to pay for everything. Too much **reliance on** a credit card is dangerous.
    - **a.** dependence on
    - **b.** debt on
    - **c.** need for

Generation Broke

1   Today's generation of college graduates is facing a financial crisis. They are starting their lives in the real world with a huge load of student loan and credit card debt. And they're struggling to manage their money in a tight job market with a rising cost of living. All of this has left the "Generation Broke" in deep financial trouble.

2   More than in previous generations, today's young adults face sharply rising college costs. In the past decade, the cost of college education in the United States has risen by nearly 40 percent. More and more college students are taking out loans or using credit cards to pay for their education. In 2006, the average student loan debt reached $14,379. An analysis by a credit research group, Experian, found that credit card debt reached an average $5,781. This type of debt is called *revolving* because the amount of debt changes every month. And larger debts like car loans averaged $17,208. This is called *installment debt* because people pay it off in monthly payments, or installments. The chart shows that these figures represent significant increases even since 2001.

3   Credit card companies now pursue college student business aggressively.[1] Credit card companies are flooding college campuses with free T-shirts, water bottles, and limited no interest fees for those who sign up. In the past, it was difficult for young adults to get credit cards. Most had to get credit cards under their parents' names or wait until they had a job. Contrast that with former student Ryan

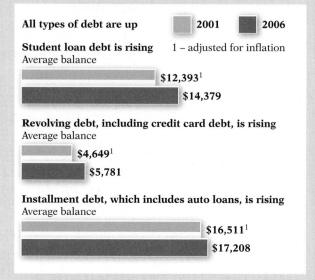

All types of debt are up	2001	2006

Student loan debt is rising   1 – adjusted for inflation
Average balance

$12,393[1]
$14,379

Revolving debt, including credit card debt, is rising
Average balance

$4,649[1]
$5,781

Installment debt, which includes auto loans, is rising
Average balance

$16,511[1]
$17,208

Peterson, 24. He accumulated $3,200 in credit card debt even before he even graduated.

4   Young adults who owe money are not handling their finances well. Experian reported that the number of late payments by this age group is rising. About half of them have stopped paying money that they owe. Like other people his age, Ryan pays only the minimum balance on his credit card every month. His debts are so high that he cannot get an auto loan. Now that Ryan has graduated and has a job, he uses a large part of his salary to pay off money he owes. Indebted adults between the ages of 18 and 24 spend almost 30 cents of every dollar earned to repay debts, according to Demos, a New York-based research group.

5   It's not surprising that high debt loads are causing anxiety. Most of today's young adults feel that they have tougher financial pressures than previous generations did. About one third

---

[1] **aggressively:** with force and determination

said they frequently worry about money. These reports came from a *USA Today* survey of young adults. "I have nightmares," said one of those surveyed. Heather Schopp, 29, has $165,000 in student loan debt.

6   Tamara Draut is the author of *Strapped: Why America's 20- and 30-Somethings Can't Get Ahead*. She reports that financial problems are giving young adults a feeling of helplessness. "It [the debt] is creating a sense that no matter what they do, they're not going to be able to **get ahead**."

7   Owing money is also affecting the career choices of young adults. Ryan Peterson majored in philosophy, but he took a job as a customer representative for an insurance company because it pays $43,000 a year. He dislikes the job, yet he must stay there to pay off the $12,000 he owes.

8   Ryan also continues to live at home even though he is working. His debts prevent him from renting or buying a home of his own. Researchers say that this **reliance on** parents is much different from that of previous generations. Young adults like Ryan depend on their parents for much longer than past generations did.

9   Financial experts consider this a social issue, not just the problem of individuals like Ryan. They say that high schools and colleges need to educate students about finance and credit. In this way, young people can begin to overcome the debt crisis facing their generation.

Identifying Main Ideas

Read each question. Circle the letter of the best answer.

1. What is the writer's overall point about young people and debt?
   a. Young people worry about their debt.
   b. Young people no longer pay their debts.
   c. Young people have student loan debt.
   d. Young people have an increasing amount of debt.

2. What is the writer's main point in paragraph 3?
   a. to explain why young people today have credit card debt
   b. to explain the credit card practices of the past generation
   c. to urge young adults not to rely on credit cards
   d. to describe one young adult's use of credit cards

3. Why does the writer present an example in paragraph 5?
   a. to explain the meaning of a person's dream
   b. to illustrate how debt can cause people to worry
   c. to persuade the reader not to get into debt
   d. to show how expensive it is to go to school

4. In paragraphs 7 and 8, what is the writer trying to show about young people and debt?

    a. Debt has caused some young people to change their careers.

    b. Debt has made some of them rely on their parents.

    c. Debt may cause some young people not to buy their own home.

    d. The writer is trying to make all of these points.

5. What is the best description for the reading?

    a. a report with facts about young people and debt

    b. a "how to" article with steps for reducing debt

    c. an opinion piece criticizing people who are in debt

    d. a comparison of debt between two generations

Identifying Details

Complete the sentences with the missing numbers, percentages, and proportions.

1. The cost of a college education in the United States has risen about _____40_____ percent in recent years.

2. The average student loan in the United States is _____.

3. Young people aged _____ to _____ spend about _____ of each dollar they earn to pay back their debts.

4. About _____ of all young adults worry about debt.

Making Inferences

What meaning can be inferred from the passage? Circle the letter of the best answer.

1. "I have nightmares," says Heather Schopp, 29, who has $165,000 in student loan debt.

    a. Heather has bad dreams about her debt.

    b. Heather has bad dreams because she is a student.

2. Most [young people in the previous generation] had to get credit cards under their parents' names or wait until they had a job. Contrast that with Ryan Peterson, 24. He accumulated $3,200 in credit card debt before he even graduated.

    a. Ryan bought things on his credit card because he could not pay cash.

    b. Ryan had a full-time job when he got his first credit card.

3. Ryan also continues to live at home even though he is working. His debts prevent him from renting or buying a home of his own.

  a. Ryan would probably prefer to live independently.

  b. Ryan would probably not prefer to live independently.

Identifying Cause and Effect in Readings

Readings often present causes or effects of a situation or condition. A reading may focus either on **cause** (the persons or things that make something happen) or **effect** (the way in which something that happens changes someone or something, or the result that something has). A reading may instead present both causes *and* effects. Use these clues to identify causes and effects:

- **Why?** As you read, look for information that tells why a situation or condition exists. The answer to the question *why* will be the cause of the situation.

  EXAMPLE

  ┌─────── SITUATION ───────┐┌─────── CAUSE ───────┐
  Many young people worry because they have high debt loads.

- **What resulted?** Look for information that tells the *result* of a situation or condition, or what happened. This information will be the *effect* of the situation.

  EXAMPLE

  ┌─────────────── SITUATION ───────────────┐
  Nearly half of 21-year-olds have stopped paying a debt.

  ┌─────────── EFFECT ───────────┐
  This forces lenders to "charge off" the debt and

  ┌─────── EFFECT ───────┐
  sell it to a collection agency.

Practice

Ryan Peterson has $12,000 in debt. Do the sentences show a cause or an effect of Ryan's financial situation? Mark each sentence C (Cause) or E (Effect).

_C_ 1. Today, many young adults get credit cards before they graduate from college.

_____ 2. Many young adults accumulate debt from college loans.

_____ 3. Many young adults worry about their debt.

_____ 4. Some young adults choose jobs they dislike because the jobs pay well.

_____ 5. Some young adults continue to live with their parents after they start working.

FROM READING TO WRITING

Journal
Choose one question and write a journal entry.

Reflecting on the Reading

Discuss the questions in pairs or small groups.

1. According to the reading, being in debt can make a person lose hope. Do you agree? Explain.
2. In general, do you think that young people spend money on unnecessary things when they don't have enough money for necessities? Explain.
3. How difficult is it to save money? Explain.

Vocabulary
For more practice with vocabulary, go to page 202.

Activating Your Vocabulary

Take notes on these questions. Try to use your answers in your Writing Assignment.

1. Does your financial situation ever feel like a **load** on your mind? Why or why not?
2. If someone did an **analysis** of your spending habits, what would they conclude?
3. Are you **struggling** with any money problems right now? Do these problems cause you **anxiety**? Explain.
4. What should you do if you're facing a money **crisis**?
5. A young person's financial **reliance on** family can be too heavy. Do you agree or disagree with this statement?

Read the model essay.

MODEL

The Broke Diaries

1   Like many college students, Angela Nissel survived on very little money before she graduated and got a job. Every aspect of her life was affected by her lack of funds. However, Angela endured the broke times with humor and creativity. She had many adventures related to food and clothing because of being broke.

2   In her book, *The Broke Diaries,* Angela describes how a lack of money affected her eating habits. Once, she had only 33 cents but remembered an advertisement for 35-cent Ramen noodles at a local store. "I put the money on the counter and quickly attempted to dash out the door with my food. The store guy called me back!" she recalled. "I should have run! I told him I thought the sign said 33 cents yesterday." In the end, the cashier let her have the noodles and told her to leave the store. Certainly, food cost was a constant challenge.

3   Being broke also affected the way that Angela dressed. One day, she tried to wash and dry her clothes. She needed six quarters, but she had only five quarters and a nickel. "I dropped my clothes into the washer and proceeded to put two quarters and a nickel into the slot," Angela wrote. "I bet this machine won't know the difference between a quarter and a nickel!" When that didn't work, she "put tape on the bottom of the nickel to make it the same height as the quarters. Still no go." Finally, she washed her clothes but had to air-dry them. Angela also wore the same clothes so often that her friends noticed. She dressed creatively on a limited budget.

4   Interestingly, Angela did not feel sad or angry about her broke years, even when she had limited food and clothing. People told her that she would look back on those times and laugh. "Thing was, I needed to laugh *while* I was broke, not later," Angela said. As a result, she posted her humorous stories on a website, and they were eventually published in a book. Now, Angela works as a writer, and she is no longer broke.

Organizing a Cause-Effect Essay

A **cause-effect essay** explains why a situation or condition happened (its *causes*) or the consequences (*effects*) of such a situation.

Use the following information to organize your cause-effect essay:

- **Introduction** Begin with general sentences to introduce the topic. Include sentences that progressively narrow to the specific thesis statement. The thesis statement should make it clear that the essay will focus on either the causes *or* effects of a situation or condition. A short essay should not present both causes and effects.

   EXAMPLE

   > She had many adventures related to food and clothing as a result of being broke.

- **Body paragraphs** The body of a cause-effect essay should explain the causes or effects of the situation. Begin the first body paragraph with a topic sentence that introduces one cause or effect.

   EXAMPLE

   > In her book, *The Broke Diaries,* Angela describes how a lack of money affected her eating habits.

   Follow the topic sentences with appropriate supporting details. Each body paragraph should explain one cause and effect.

- **Conclusion** Conclude with a paragraph that restates the causes or effects of the situation or condition that you are writing about.

Practice

A. Read the essay "The Broke Diaries" again. Then answer these questions.

1. What is the situation or condition that the writer is presenting?

   _____

2. Does the essay focus on *causes* or *effects*?

   _____

3. What are some of the *causes* or *effects* presented in the essay?

   _____

   _____

   _____

B. Complete this outline for "The Broke Diaries." Note that a supporting point can be an example or a story that illustrates the topic sentence.

Outline for "The Broke Diaries"

I. Introduction

    Thesis statement: <u>Angela faced many adventures relating to food and</u>

    <u>clothing as a result of being broke.</u>

II. Body paragraph 1

    Topic sentence: _____

    _____

      A. Supporting point 1: _____

      _____

III. Body paragraph 2

    Topic sentence: _____

    _____

      A. Supporting point 1: _____

      _____

      B. Supporting point 2: _____

      _____

IV. Conclusion

    Restatement of thesis statement: _____

    _____

C. Check your outline for omissions or mistakes. Work alone or in pairs.

- Does each body paragraph explain a part of the thesis statement?
- Does each body paragraph have appropriate supporting points?
- Does the conclusion restate the thesis statement?

WRITING SKILL

Writing a Proposal

Read the model essay proposal.

MODEL

> I plan to write an essay about common effects of a shaky financial situation on a person's life. The effects include (1) running up personal debt by borrowing from friends, (2) heavy reliance on credit cards, and (3) anxiety. I will support my thesis statement with statistics from the reading, "Generation Broke," and personal experiences (mine and my friends').

In many writing-intensive college courses, you are required to submit a proposal for an essay you will write. A **proposal** is an informal explanation or summary of what you plan to write about. A proposal should include the main idea of your essay and the supporting points you will include.

Practice

A. *Write a thesis statement for the proposed essay, using the information from the model proposal above. Compare your statement with a partner's.*

_____

_____

B. *On a separate sheet of paper, write a simple outline for the same essay. Include topic sentences for the body paragraphs and at least two supporting points that could be included in each body paragraph. Compare your outlines in small groups.*

WRITING ASSIGNMENT

Write a thesis statement, proposal, and outline for a cause-effect essay. Follow the steps.

STEP 1   Get ideas.

A. Choose a topic for your proposal. Check (✔) it. You will write an essay on this topic in Chapter 12.

❑ **Topic 1:** A person's financial situation

❑ **Topic 2:** A person's spending habits

B. The chart below lists words that describe each topic. Write additional descriptors for each topic and discuss them in a group.

Topic 1: Financial Situation	Topic 2: Spending Habits
unstable	careful
solid	careless

STEP 2   Organize your ideas.

    A. Make a cause-effect chart like the one shown below to help you focus on either the causes or the effects of your topic.

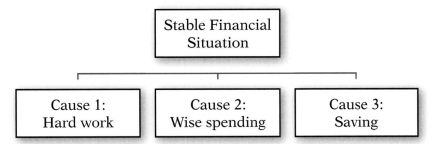

    B. Write an effective thesis statement for your topic.

    EXAMPLE

      My friend Nora is financially stable because she works hard, spends wisely, and saves money.

    C. Next, make an outline for the essay you will write, using the model on page 125. Include your thesis statement.

STEP 3   Write a rough draft.

Write your proposal. Use the information from Steps 1 and 2. Include vocabulary from the chapter where possible.

STEP 4   Revise your rough draft.

Read your proposal. Use the Writing Checklist to look for mistakes.

Writing Checklist

❏ Does the thesis statement make it clear that the essay will present *causes* or *effects* of a situation or condition?

❏ Does the proposal include the main idea of your essay?

❏ Does the proposal describe the supporting points that you will include in your essay?

❏ Does your outline follow the model outline on page 125?

STEP 5   Edit your writing.

A. Edit your proposal. Correct any mistakes in capitalization, punctuation, spelling, or verb use.

B. Exchange proposals with a partner. Use the Correction Symbols on page 191 to mark each other's work.

EXAMPLE

Malls have had a negative effect on smaller shopping districts in my

PUNCTUATION ERROR (P)
. They
city, they take away their business.

STEP 6   Write a final copy.

Correct your mistakes. Copy your final work and give it to your instructor.

The IKEA Success Story

PRE-READING

Discussion

Discuss the questions in pairs or small groups.

1. Look at the photograph. What do you know about IKEA stores?
2. Think of the most popular stores in your community. Why are they popular?
3. What are the most successful types of stores in your community? Explain.

Vocabulary

Read the sentences. Match the boldfaced words with the definitions.

__b__ 1. Shoppers were **eager** to visit the new Wegmann's grocery store when it opened near our home.

____ 2. **Consumers** in the United States can compare different brands of products by reading the magazine *Consumer Reports*.

____ 3. Barnes & Noble decided to **expand** its business by selling books online in addition to its store locations.

____ 4. Apple Corporation has **stimulated** its business through strong sales of its iPod music-playing and storage device.

____ 5. The fruit market on Broad Street is always crowded because other stores **can't beat** its prices and selection.

____ 6. Food stores **cleverly** place candy next to cash registers so that children will see it.

____ 7. The Richmond Museum in Vancouver has held several **exhibitions** of historical items from 18th and 19th century Canadian businesses.

____ 8. It's easy to buy items that you don't need if you **wander** through a store.

____ 9. Trader Joe's, a specialty food store, tries to **engage** customer interest with advertisements that describe its food humorously.

____ 10. Walmart is an international retail business **based** in Bentonville, Arkansas. The company grew from one small store there.

---

a. not be able to do better than
b. wanting to do something very much
c. the people who buy or use goods and services
d. make someone interested in something
e. walk around an area without a clear direction or purpose
f. in an intelligent and skillful way
g. use a city or town as your main place of business or activities
h. become larger in size, area, activity, or number
i. encourage more of an activity
j. public shows where you put things so people can see them

The IKEA Success Story

1   Days before IKEA opened in West Chester, Ohio, in March of 2008, fans of this Swedish home furnishings store were camping outside, awaiting the store opening. On the big day, tens of thousands of eager consumers filled Ohio's first IKEA store, the 34th in the United States. Many drove miles to get there, and some even took time off from work. Like many Ohioans, more than 500 million people shop at more than 270 IKEA stores in 36 countries, buying nearly US$30 billion in home furnishings in 2008. How did this business expand from a small roadside stand in a Swedish town to one of the world's leading retailers? Intelligent design and a customer-focused shopping experience have stimulated IKEA's business.

2   From the start, company founder Ingvar Kamprad (the "I" and "K" in IKEA) has aimed to create functional, low-priced, yet elegant products, an idea that's central to IKEA's success. Kamprad began selling cards and seeds at age 17. In 1955, he decided to design his own furniture so that it would be more useful, attractive, and cost-effective than other furniture. An example is IKEA's popular Poäng armchair, which has a cotton cover, sleek wooden frame, and 25-year warranty, and sells for US$89.99. The company gave away 100 Poäng chairs to early-bird customers on opening day in West Chester. Like other IKEA furniture, the chair is "flat packed" to keep prices low. Customers don't seem to mind the do-it-yourself assembly,[1] especially since many feel that they can't beat the prices on IKEA designs. One shopper at the West Chester IKEA bought a sleek, silver-colored steel shelf unit for US$19.99. "I really wanted these shelves. They're interlocking, they're a good price, good quality," he said.

3   In addition, IKEA makes shopping enjoyable. In stores, the experience begins at the front door, where bright blue and yellow signs guide customers to pick up shopping bags, tape measures, pencils, and notepads. Cleverly designed paths lead shoppers through the huge space (344,000 square feet in West Chester). The store is filled with "furniture exhibitions"—rooms set up with furniture and eye-catching textiles, lighting, rugs, and art. Shoppers feel free to wander through the spaces, sitting and even lying down on furniture. Some are looking through their IKEA catalogs or taking notes as they consider how the furnishings will work in their own homes. The pieces fit so well together, it's not uncommon for a customer like Jen Segrest, founder of the OH, IKEA web log,[2] to fill every room in the house with IKEA products. Additional features of IKEA stores encourage customers to spend an average of two to three hours there. There's a restaurant with Swedish dishes, a snack bar and Swedish food shop, and a supervised children's play area. Similarly, IKEA's annual catalog draws customers with photos of coordinated[3] room settings and appealing text that asks: "Like

(continued)

---

[1] **assembly:** the process of putting something together

[2] **web log:** A web log, or *blog,* is a journal available on the Internet

[3] **coordinated:** matched by choice so everything works together well

having friends over but don't have a big home?" or "What's the secret to fitting all your things into a small space?" IKEA's stores and catalogs definitely aim to attract and engage customers.

5   Of course, there are many other low-cost furniture retailers. Yet IKEA is unique. The company has created a strong base of customers drawn to its low prices, European styles, and appealing stores and catalogs. With a new store in Ohio and other U.S. locations expected, IKEA is likely to continue to grow beyond its European-based market.

Identifying Main Ideas

Match the beginning of each sentence with an ending. Then circle the number of the sentence that represents the main idea of the reading.

_____ 1. The man who started the company

_____ 2. People enjoy shopping at IKEA because the stores

_____ 3. IKEA is one-of-a kind

_____ 4. IKEA stores are successful because

a. and will likely keep growing.
b. they have an intelligent design and focus on customers.
c. have an appealing design that invites customers to sit and lie on the furniture.
d. wanted to create low-cost, useful products that look nice.

Identifying Details

Match each feature of the IKEA stores with a description. Check your answers in pairs.

Features

_____ 1. Flat-packed goods

_____ 2. Signs and paths

_____ 3. Furniture exhibitions

_____ 4. Added features like a restaurant

_____ 5. The annual catalog

Description

a. show products in room settings.

b. encourage shoppers to stay longer.

c. keep prices low.

d. has photographs of products.

e. guide customers through the store.

Making Inferences

What meaning can be inferred from the passage? Circle the letter of the best answer.

1. Kamprad began selling cards and seeds at age 17. In 1955, he decided to design his own furniture so that it would be more useful, attractive, and cost-effective than other furniture.

   a. Kamprad did not sell furniture before 1955.

   b. Kamprad may have sold furniture before 1955.

2. Like other IKEA furniture, the chair is "flat packed" to keep prices low. Customers don't seem to mind the do-it-yourself assembly, especially since many feel that they can't beat the prices on IKEA designs.

   a. IKEA furniture is sold in boxes.

   b. IKEA furniture is sold assembled.

3. Similarly, IKEA's annual catalog draws customers with photos of coordinated room settings and appealing text that asks: "Like having friends over but don't have a big home?" or "What's the secret to fitting all your things into a small space?"

   a. IKEA wants to attract customers with large houses.

   b. IKEA wants to attract customers with small houses.

FROM READING TO WRITING

Journal
Choose one question and write a journal entry.

Reflecting on the Reading

Discuss the questions in pairs or small groups.

1. Think of examples of successful stores. Are low prices the greatest factor in the success of a store? Are there other reasons why a store succeeds?
2. If you know that a store has a pleasant environment, does that influence whether you shop at that store? Explain.
3. Do you shop by catalogs or online? If so, explain in what cases you buy from a catalog or an online seller.

Vocabulary
For more practice with vocabulary, go to page 203.

Activating Your Vocabulary

Take notes on these questions. Try to use your answers in your Writing Assignment.

1. Which stores in your community have prices that other stores **can't beat**? Do you shop in those stores? Why or why not?
2. Have you ever managed your money **cleverly**? Explain.

3. How can **consumers** improve their spending habits?
4. Some people like to shop and some people don't. Are you an **eager** or reluctant shopper?
5. Has you savings **expanded** or shrunk over the past five years. Explain.

WRITING

WRITING SKILL

Using Hedging Words

Learning to use words to hedge, or limit, the strength of general statements will help you express ideas more accurately when you write.

Look for these common types of **hedging words**:

- **Modal auxiliary verbs that limit the strength of verbs:** These modal verbs show possibility, not certainty: *can, may, might.*

  EXAMPLE

  A full-time food store cashier **might** not be able to support a family on his or her paycheck.

- **Adverbs that limit the strength of verbs and adjectives:** Adverbs such as *sometimes*, *usually*, or *often* show how frequently the action or condition occurs.

  EXAMPLE

  IKEA stores are **often** crowded on the weekends.

- **Quantifiers that limit the strength of nouns:** Without quantifiers such as *many*, *most*, and *some*, the noun includes all members of the group. For example, *countries* means all countries.

  EXAMPLE

  Some countries have one or more IKEA stores.

Practice

A. *Circle the letter of the word or phrase that best completes each sentence. More than one correct answer is possible.*

1. Housing is _____ a person's biggest expense.
   a. always　　　　　b. sometimes　　　　　c. usually

2. _____ people waste money on food.
   a. Many　　　　　b. Most　　　　　c. Some

3. Young people _____ spend too much money on clothing.
   a. often　　　　　b. sometimes　　　　　c. always

4. College students ____ get into debt from student loans.

    a. may   **b.** can   **c.** might

5. ____ college students work in low-paying jobs.

    a. Many   **b.** Most   **c.** Few

B. Read the proposal for a cause-effect essay. Revise it by adding appropriate hedging words. Discuss your answers in pairs.

Proposal: The Causes of Careless Spending

I plan to write an essay about how young people today do not watch how they spend money. My main point will be that young people spend money on useless and expensive goods and services. First, I will explain how young people pay for unnecessary items such as cable television and video rentals. In addition, I'll describe how they do not think when they spend money at expensive restaurants or clothing stores. Through these supporting ideas, I will explain how young people spend money carelessly.

WRITING ASSIGNMENT

Write a cause-effect essay using your proposal and outline from Chapter 11. Follow the steps to complete your essay.

STEP 1   **Get ideas.**

    A. Read over the proposal and outline that you wrote in Chapter 11. Make sure that they follow the examples on page 125 and include two or three causes or effects about the topic. Make any necessary changes.

    B. Next, present your proposal and outline in a small group. Explain your thesis statement.

    C. Work with the group to get ideas for the introduction paragraph of your essay. Take notes on the suggestions.

    EXAMPLE

        Like other students at her college, Tanika Edwards works part-time while she studies. Her living expenses are high, but Tanika's schedule prevents her from working full-time. Her busy schedule, full-time student status, and low-paying job have all contributed to her shaky financial situation.

STEP 2   Organize your ideas.

A. Revise the outline of your essay, using the ideas from Step 1.

B. Next, write a rough draft of your introduction paragraph, using the ideas from Step 1. Be sure to include an introduction to the topic and a thesis statement.

C. Show your proposal, outline, and introduction to your instructor before you write your essay.

STEP 3   Write a rough draft.

Write your essay. Include vocabulary from the chapter where possible.

STEP 4   Revise your rough draft.

Read your paragraph. Use the Writing Checklist to look for mistakes. Work alone or in pairs.

Writing Checklist

❑ Does the introduction introduce the topic and include your thesis statement?

❑ Does your essay follow the suggested outline for organizing a cause-effect essay?

❑ Does each body paragraph present a cause or an effect of the topic?

❑ Did you use hedging words appropriately?

❑ Did you use vocabulary from the chapter appropriately?

STEP 5   Edit your writing.

A. Edit your essay. Correct any mistakes in capitalization, punctuation, spelling, or verb use.

B. Exchange essays with a partner. Use the Correction Symbols on page 191 to mark each other's work.

EXAMPLE

MISSING WORD ERROR (O)

so
People should save money,˄they have to spend carefully.

STEP 6   Write a final copy.

Correct your mistakes. Copy your final essay and give it to your instructor.

UNIT SEVEN

Generations

The Newest Generation at Work

Generation Y worker

PRE-READING

Discussion

Discuss the questions in pairs or small groups.

1. Look at the photograph on page 137. How many generations do you see? Which generation most closely matches your age group?
2. What characteristics do you value in a job? Rank these characteristics from 1 (most important) to 4 (least important).

   _____ **a.** meaningful job   _____ **c.** high salary

   _____ **b.** flexible schedule   _____ **d.** friendly workplace

3. The reading in this chapter mentions three generations: the baby boomers (born 1946–1964), Generation X (born 1965–1975), and Generation Y (born 1976–1990s). Do you think these generations would agree with your rankings in Exercise 2? Explain.

Vocabulary

Read the boldfaced words and their definitions. Then complete each sentence with the correct word or phrase.

accommodate:	do what someone wants or needs in order to help or satisfy that person
adapt:	change a behavior or ideas to fit a new situation
eventually:	after a long time
motivator:	a thing, action, or person that causes you to want to do or achieve something
permanent:	continuing to exist for a long time or for always
promotion:	a move to a better, more responsible position at work
retain:	keep something or continue to have something
stable:	steady or secure and not likely to move or change
stick with:	continue doing something or supporting someone
transition:	change from one form or condition to another

1. The clock on the wall is _____*stable*_____. It doesn't look like it's going to fall.

2. Patricia has to re-apply for her job every year. It's not a _____ position.

3. If you want to _____ new vocabulary words, you must study and use them often. Otherwise, you'll forget them.

4. Many buildings today _____ handicapped people by providing ramps and elevators to increase accessibility.

5. What is a greater _____ for you in choosing a job: money or enjoyment of the work?

6. Tom is a salesman, and he has applied for a manager's position. If he gets the _____, he'll earn more money.

7. Many changes have occurred in technological devices. Some people believe that _____ we will use one device to do everything.

8. Can you _____ to using new technology, like a new cell phone? Or do you prefer to use older technology?

9. Michael now goes to school all year long. He found it difficult to _____ to the new schedule.

10. Alma is very determined. She _____ a task even when it takes a lot of time and effort.

The Newest Generation at Work

1   At 24, Dave Townsend is one of 76 million Generation Y members. He works alongside two other generations—85 million baby boomers and 50 million Generation Xers. Dave and his peers differ from previous generations of workers. While older workers juggle work and family demands, few Generation Yers have families or children. Most don't need to **accommodate** work and family like the other two groups. Yet Generation Y members have strong ideas about what satisfies them. This newest generation of workers is making career decisions based on personal values and preferences.

2   More than half of Generation Yers live with their parents after they finish college, so they have more choices about work than previous generations did. They can choose jobs that pay less but give them personal benefits. Elizabeth Ruffino, 23, holds a master's degree in art history, and she works as a part-time college teacher. She lives with her parents, so she manages on two part-time salaries while she finishes her doctorate degree. But part-time teaching doesn't pay as well as a **permanent**, full-time position. **Eventually**, Elizabeth will seek a more **stable** job. Meantime, she takes summer vacations with friends and even saves money while working. And she enjoys what she's doing.

3   Many Generation Y workers switch jobs because they want to do meaningful work, not just work that pays well. Dave has nearly completed his bachelor's degree in history, but he quit a $35,000 job as a customer service representative for a leading insurance company. He did not feel he was helping people. Now he works full-time as a teacher's aide at a private high school for troubled youth, earning $12 per hour. He can barely pay his bills, even living with his parents. But Dave loves the work and feels that he is doing something worthwhile. He talks about getting a second job or returning to work at the insurance company. But he **sticks with** the teaching job because of the satisfaction that he gets from helping students.

4   Friendship is also a strong **motivator** for Generation Y members. Young workers may seek work in places that support friendship. Rebecca Thomas earns about $28,000 a year managing a health-food supermarket. Her salary doesn't leave her with much extra money, but the store is an informal, friendly workplace. With an associate's degree in business administration, she likely could earn more money at a more traditional company. But Rebecca likes the friends she has made at the store and does not

want to change jobs. She started as a cashier while she was still in school, and she's worked her way to an assistant store manager.

5   Like Rebecca, Generation Y workers are also looking for jobs where they can grow professionally. Another reason that Dave left his insurance job was because the company didn't offer him opportunities for **promotion**. Similarly, the financial advising firm Deloitte found that there was a high turnover among its youngest workers. They hired Stan Smith to study the problem. Smith told *Time* magazine that young workers leave a company when they see no other choices.

"Two-thirds of the people who left Deloitte left to do something they could have done with us, but we made it difficult for them to **transition**." So Smith is now trying to **retain** Generation Y workers at Deloitte by helping them plan their careers.

6   In the near future, Generation Y workers will be running the workplace. This new generation will reshape the business world. Consequently, companies should learn to **adapt** to Generation Y work values and preferences. And older workers should try to understand the values of their newest co-workers.

Identifying Main Ideas

Match each person with the main idea he or she illustrates.

_____ 1. Elizabeth Ruffino

_____ 2. Dave Townsend

_____ 3. Rebecca Thomas

_____ 4. Stan Smith

a. Generation Y members often choose jobs where they can socialize and make friends.

b. Many people of Generation Y live with their parents after they go to college.

c. Some employers help Generation Y workers plan their careers so they will stay at their jobs.

d. Generation Y workers sometimes choose work that is meaningful over work that pays well.

Identifying Details

Match each description of Generation Y workers with a result.

Generation Y workers . . .   **Result**

_____ 1. want meaningful work.

_____ 2. prefer not to change jobs often.

_____ 3. often live with parents.

_____ 4. value a friendly workplace.

_____ 5. will one day run companies.

a. Companies help employees make career moves.

b. Workers choose jobs where they can help people.

c. Older workers should learn about the values of younger workers.

d. Workers don't have to choose high-paying jobs.

e. Workers may stay in a job where the co-workers have good relations.

Making Inferences

The following information is not directly stated in the reading. Infer what the writer would say is true. Check (✔) each statement that the writer would agree with.

_____ 1. Children and family are less important to Generation Yers than to the other two generations.

_____ 2. Many companies are unsuccessful in keeping Generation Y employees.

_____ 3. Generation Yers care less about high salaries than previous generations.

_____ 4. Baby boomers and Generation Xers have the same values as Generation Yers.

READING SKILL

Distinguishing Generalizations from Support

Writers often present **generalizations**, or general statements of truth, about subjects. Then writers support these statements with facts, reasons, or examples to show that the generalizations are true.

These tips will help you distinguish generalizations from support:

- **Generalizations** present opinions or statements of belief that most people agree with. Strong generalizations generally use simple or future verb tenses. As you learned in Chapter 12, writers limit the strength of generalizations by using hedging words like *may*.

  EXAMPLES

  Generation Y workers will choose a job just to be with their friends.

  Generation Y workers may prefer to work away from the office.

- **Supporting sentences** present specific information. Look for names, numbers, or descriptive or narrative details.

  EXAMPLE

  Rebecca Thomas earns about $28,000 a year managing a health-food supermarket.

Practice

Scan the reading to find these sentences. Is each sentence a generalization or a supporting detail? Mark G *(Generalization) or* SD *(Supporting Detail).*

_____ 1. Generation Y members have strong ideas about what satisfies them.

_____ 2. More than half of Generation Yers live with their parents after they finish college, so they have more choices about work than previous generations.

_____ 3. Dave has nearly completed his bachelor's degree in history, but he quit a $35,000 job as a customer service representative for a leading insurance company to go back to school.

_____ 4. "Two-thirds of the people who left Deloitte left to do something they could have done with us, but we made it difficult for them to transition."

_____ 5. Friendship is also a strong motivator for Generation Y members.

FROM READING TO WRITING

Journal
Choose one question and write a journal entry.

Reflecting on the Reading

Discuss the questions in pairs or small groups.

1. What do you think Generation Yers mean when they say they want to do *meaningful* work? What are some examples?
2. What are the characteristics of your ideal job?
3. Think of your own or someone else's job experience. How did you (or that person) balance work, school, and/or family responsibilities?

Vocabulary
For more
practice with
vocabulary, go
to page 204.

Activating Your Vocabulary

Take notes on these questions. Try to use your answers in your Writing Assignment.

1. What is the greatest **motivator** for you to get a new job or new place to live?
2. Give one example of a **stable** job or a stable living situation.
3. Should an employer **accommodate** a worker's family responsibilities? If so, in what ways?
4. Which are the most effective ways for a company to **retain** its employees?
5. How might a worker **adapt** to a new boss? How might a person **adapt** to a new roommate?

WRITING

Read the model essay.

MODEL

The Case for Telecommuting

Technology continues to advance, but most of us still work at traditional job sites. However, more and more people are *telecommuting*. They often work from home using a phone and/or a computer. Telecommuting is most commonly found in the information industries. These include computer programming, sales, education, and accounting. Many companies in these areas think that telecommuting works better than the traditional work model.

First, telecommuters save time and money. That's because they do not have to travel to and from work. In contrast, traditional workers contribute to morning and evening rush hour problems. They add to traffic jams and air pollution. They also spend money on gasoline and time to travel to and from work. On the other hand, telecommuters do all or part of their work from home. They can spend their saved time productively on work- or home-related tasks. Telecommuters frequently use the extra time on family, work, and personal errands.

Moreover, "telework" provides employment opportunities for people who might otherwise be unable to work. Disabled workers, parents, or people in rural areas sometimes cannot work at traditional workplaces. They may have physical problems, or they may need to care for others. They may also live in remote locations. In contrast, telecommuters do not need to travel regularly to a workplace. By telecommuting, the disabled, the elderly, rural workers, and people with families can work from home. For instance, a wheelchair-bound instructor can teach an online course. A parent of pre-school children can make sales by using a computer or telephone.

In the future, researchers need to study carefully this newer way of working. Does it increase productivity and motivation? Can it save companies money? Supporters believe that telecommuting has these additional benefits. But there is little research to prove their claims. For now, the growing number of telecommuters shows that telework has become a valuable part of the working world.

WRITING SKILL

Organizing a Comparison-Contrast Essay

When writers want to decide between options, they compare or contrast. They **compare** subjects to show similarities. They **contrast** subjects to show differences. Writers may also conclude that they prefer one subject over another.

The model essay, "The Case for Telecommuting," compares traditional work and telework. Here's how it is organized:

- **Introduction and thesis statement** The introduction paragraph presents a thesis statement with the writer's conclusion that Subject B (telecommuting) is preferable to Subject A (traditional work).

  EXAMPLE

  > Many companies in these areas think that telecommuting works better than the traditional work model.

- **Body paragraphs** The essay follows the common point-by-point pattern for organizing comparison-contrast essays. Each paragraph presents one point, or key feature, about Subject A (traditional work) and the same point about Subject B (telework). The essay follows this pattern twice because it presents two points about the subjects.

- **Conclusion** The conclusion includes a sentence to restate the thesis statement and one option for closing an essay: a prediction and recommendation about the future.

Practice

Read the model essay again and complete the outline below. Work in pairs and compare your answers.

Outline for "The Case for Telecommuting"

I. Introduction

Thesis statement: *Many companies in these areas think that telecommuting works better than the traditional work model.*

II. Body paragraph 1

Point of comparison 1: Time and money

Topic sentence: *First, telecommuters save time and money.*

    1. Support: Subject A (traditional work)

        1. _____

        2. _____

        3. _____

    2. Support: Subject B (telecommuting)

        1. _____

        2. _____

        3. _____

III. Body paragraph 2

Point of comparison 2: Employment opportunities

Topic sentence: _____

_____

    3. Support: Subject A (traditional work)

        1. _____

        2. _____

    4. Support: Subject B (telecommuting)

        1. _____

        2. _____

IV. Conclusion

Restatement of thesis: _____

_____

WRITING ASSIGNMENT

Write a thesis statement, proposal, and outline for a compare-contrast essay. Follow the steps.

STEP 1   **Get ideas.**

A. Choose a topic for your proposal. Check (✔) it. You will write an essay on this topic in Chapter 14.

❏ **Topic 1:** A comparison of two work situations

❏ **Topic 2:** A comparison of two living situations

B. Brainstorm a list of pairs of subjects to compare. Use the lists below for ideas. Add your own ideas to the lists.

Topic 1: Work Situations

Working in one type of job versus another type

Working in one culture versus another culture

Working in an English-speaking environment versus a non-English-speaking environment

Working _____ versus _____

Topic 2: Living Situations

Living independently versus living with a roommate

Living in an apartment versus living in a single home

Living in a city versus living in the suburbs

Living _____ versus _____

C. Choose two subjects from your list to compare and contrast.

D. Brainstorm the similarities and differences of your subjects and write them in a chart. Then choose whether your essay will focus on similarities or differences.

Living in a city versus living in the suburbs

Similarities	*Differences*	
	City	*Suburbs*
Have neighbors		
Must pay for rent	*Close to shops*	*Must drive to shop*
Must pay utilities	*Close to work*	*Far from work*
	Lots of noise	*Very quiet*
	Exciting	*Boring*
	Less safe	*Safer*

I choose to focus my essay on <u>differences</u> .

STEP 2 Organize your ideas.

Write a thesis statement that names the two subjects and states if you are comparing differences or similarities.

EXAMPLE

Although many people prefer suburban living, living in the city is more convenient and exciting.

STEP 3 Write a rough draft.

Write your proposal and outline. Use the guidelines on pages 124 and 145. Include vocabulary from the chapter where possible.

EXAMPLE

I plan to write about living in the city versus living in the suburbs. I will focus on differences. Living in the city is preferable because of the convenience and the excitement.

STEP 4 Revise your rough draft.

Read your proposal and outline. Use the Writing Checklist to look for mistakes. Work alone or in pairs.

Writing Checklist

❑ Does the proposal present a plan for what you will write about?

❑ Does it include the main idea of your essay?

❑ Does your thesis statement introduce the two subjects that you are comparing or contrasting?

❑ Does the thesis statement make it clear that the essay will present either differences or similarities?

❑ Does your outline follow the model outline on pages 145–146?

❑ Did you use vocabulary from the chapter appropriately?

STEP 5 Edit your writing.

A. Edit your proposal and outline. Correct any mistakes in capitalization, punctuation, spelling, or verb use.

B. Exchange proposals and outlines with a partner. Use the Correction Symbols on page 191 to mark each other's work.

EXAMPLE

CAPITALIZATION ERROR

c

Another advantage of living in the Çity is the convenient location.

STEP 6 Write a final copy.

Correct your mistakes. Copy your final work and give it to your instructor.

Vocabulary

Read the boldfaced words and their definitions. Then complete the paragraph with the correct word or phrase.

arrangement:	something that has been agreed on
chances are:	it is likely that
cite:	mention something as an example or proof of something else
count on:	depend on someone or something
fashionable:	popular, especially for a short time
incidence:	the number of times something happens
roots:	the origins of a custom or tradition that has continued for a long time
statistics:	a collection of numbers that represent facts or measurements

Gen Y Dorm Rooms

In their college days, many baby boomers decorated their dormitory rooms *on the cheap*. They used second-hand goods from their parents' attics or thrift stores. This (**1**) ___*arrangement*___ worked for some Generation Xers, too. But now Generation Yers are in college. Dormitory decoration has become big business. (**2**) _____, if you visit a Gen Y dormitory nowadays, you'll find a different scene. You'll see flat-screen TVs, color-coordinated linens, and other expensive items. Both male and female students are purchasing (**3**) _____ items like comforters and curtains. In fact, recent (**4**) _____ indicate that for every $10 that Gen Yers spend on college, $1 goes to decorate dorms. It's not surprising, then, to see so many companies targeting advertisements at college students. What are the (**5**) _____ of the change? Researchers (**6**) _____ big retail companies like Target, IKEA, and Walmart. They have helped make "back-to-college" the second largest shopping season of the year. Retailers ignored the college market for years. But now the (**7**) _____ of special advertising campaigns just before the fall semester starts is increasing. Clearly, you can (**8**) _____ Gen Y college students to keep this "back to college" decorating trend in full swing.

Staying Home with Momma

An Italian man and his mother

PRE-READING

Discussion

Discuss the questions in pairs or small groups.

1. Look at the photograph. Can you guess what kind of relationship the young man and his mother may have?
2. Do you think single young adults should live at home or on their own? Why or why not?
3. At what age do you think it may be appropriate for a young adult to live independently? Explain.

Staying Home with Momma

By Carla Power, Newsweek

1   ROME, Italy—Jesus Emiliano Coltorti, a 25-year-old Roman actor, would love to move out of his mother's apartment in the city's **fashionable** Trastevere district and get his own place. His mother knows it, too. "I understand he's grown up and he will go away sometime," sighs Paola Sechi. "I just don't want to lose him."

2   **Chances are**, she won't. More than 70 percent of Italian sons under 30 live with their parents. And when Italian children do move out, they don't go far. Nearly 43 percent of Italians between 18 and 64 live within a kilometer of their mothers. Street-corner sociologists make fun of the stay-at-home-with-mamma phenomenon as *il mammismo*, or "mamma's boy syndrome."[1] They **cite** the culture of the strong Italian family—the overbearing mother and overprotected son—as a reason for the rising **incidence** of *mammismo*.

3   But its real **roots** are economic. Rents and unemployment among Italy's young are high. As a result, Italian children are staying at home with their parents longer. In 1990 about 52 percent of Italians from 18 to 34 lived with their parents. In 1998 the percentage rose to nearly 59 percent. "Everyone I know would live alone if they could," says Raffaella Diamanti, a 33-year-old theater designer. "But the economy doesn't give them the chance."

4   Not yet, anyway. Italy is a country where youth unemployment stays around 24 percent. Most of the jobs available for Italians in their 20s and 30s are temporary ones. They lack social benefits and job security. The average job hunt for young Italian adults takes about four years. This is according to ISTAT, Italy's national **statistics** institute. White-collar professionals like teachers and architects can expect to make about 675 Euros or US $955 a month. So it's not surprising that in big cities like Rome or Milan, where the smallest apartments can run 400 to 500 Euros a month, few twenty-somethings move out.

5   Most accept their situation. Most commonly, young people are happy with the living **arrangement**. "Their mothers service them and their fathers support them," says Chiara Saraceno, a social-science professor at the University of Torino. Marcello Magnano, a 34-year-old cab driver who lived at home until he married at 27, remembers that, thanks to his mother, "I did nothing at home—just made my bed."

6   With in-house service like that, why move out? Most universities don't have dormitories, so there's no place to go during college. Nor is there a tradition of roughing it[2] as a poor student: "The idea that you might have a lower standard of living while you're studying isn't a part of youth culture in Italy," says Saraceno. And there's a cultural shame against moving out. Unless you live in the sticks where there is no university nearby, leaving your family to work or study is not acceptable to Italians. "People will say that something is wrong with your family or your

(continued)

---

[1] **syndrome:** a set of mental or physical characteristics that show that you have a condition

[2] **roughing it:** informal, living in conditions that are not very comfortable

relationship," says Saraceno. The only legitimate reason to leave the family is marriage. And this is something Italians are doing later and later.

7   Once they do marry and raise a family, women often end up caring not only for their children but for their parents as well. Daughters, in particular, serve as social security for their aging mothers. Fifty-eight percent of grown Italian sons and 69 percent of daughters with sick mothers see them several times weekly. Mostly women make up for the state's lack of social benefits. They care for unemployed sons or nurse sick or aging parents. "There's a mommy economy at work in Italy, and there's a daughter economy, too," notes Linda Laura Sabbadini, director of research at ISTAT. Italian women may lose hope at having to care for their children even after they're grown. But at least they can **count on** someone taking care of them when they get old.

Identifying Main Ideas

Read each question. Circle the letter of the best answer.

1. What is the main idea of the reading?
   a. Italian sons tend to live close to their mothers' home.
   b. Italian sons increasingly continue to live with their mothers.
   c. Italian sons prefer to live in fashionable neighborhoods.
   d. Italian sons prefer living with their mothers to living on their own.

2. What is the writer's main purpose in paragraph 1?
   a. To persuade readers that sons should not live independently.
   b. To explain why mothers want their sons to remain at home.
   c. To identify the most fashionable district of Rome.
   d. To present an example of a stay-at-home Italian son.

3. According to paragraphs 2–4, why do Italian sons continue to live with their mothers?
   a. They are "mamma's boys."
   b. They do not want to live alone.
   c. They cannot afford to live alone.
   d. All of the above are true.

4. According to paragraph 6, what does the Italian culture say about students living away from home?
   a. It's not acceptable for married women.
   b. It's acceptable if you live in a dormitory.
   c. It's acceptable if you live far from a university.
   d. It's unacceptable in all situations.

5. In Italy, what family responsibilities do adult daughters have?

    a. They see their old or sick parents regularly.

    b. They do more housework than males do.

    c. They only care for their own children.

    d. All of the above are true.

Identifying Details

Complete the sentences with the correct numbers and percentages.

1. More than ____ percent of Italian sons under age ____ live with their parents.

2. Almost ____ percent of Italians live within one kilometer of their parents.

3. In 1998, nearly ____ percent of Italians between the ages of ____ and ____ lived with their parents.

4. Youth unemployment in Italy is about ____ percent.

5. About ____ percent of grown Italian daughters visit their sick mothers several times a week.

Making Inferences

What meaning can be inferred from the statement? Answer the question.

1. When Italian children do move out, they don't go far.

    What does the writer imply occurs in other countries?

    _____

    _____

2. Street-corner sociologists make fun of the stay-at-home-with-mamma phenomenon.

    Why does the writer use the words "make fun of"? What is she implying about this situation?

    _____

    _____

3. Most of the jobs available for Italians in their 20s and 30s are temporary ones. They lack social benefits and job security.

   What is the writer implying about the economic situation in Italy?

   _____

   _____

4. Daughters, in particular, serve as social security for their aging mothers. Mostly women make up for the state's lack of social benefits. They care for unemployed sons or nurse sick or aging parents.

   What does the writer imply about the Italian government?

   _____

   _____

FROM READING TO WRITING

Reflecting on the Reading

Journal
Choose one question and write a journal entry.

Discuss the questions in pairs or small groups.

1. Which of these living arrangements suits you the best: living at home with parents, living independently, or living with a roommate? Explain.
2. How does the living situation of young adults in Italy differ from the situation in another country that you know?
3. How would you like to change your living arrangement?

Activating Your Vocabulary

Vocabulary
For more practice with vocabulary, go to page 205.

Take notes on these questions. Try to use your answers in your Writing Assignment.

1. What do you think the **chances are** that college graduates near you may have difficulty finding jobs or moving away from home?
2. Who can you **count on** to help you find a good job or a new place to live?
3. Is it easy for young people to afford housing in **fashionable** areas of your community? Explain.
4. Is there a rising **incidence** of unemployment in your community? If so, what do you think are the **roots** of the problem?
5. In five years, do you expect to have the same job or living **arrangement** that you have now? Explain.

Read the model essay.

MODEL

Two Hot Tech Cities

The landscapes of Austin, Texas, and Phoenix, Arizona, look very different. Austin has rolling green hills and rivers. Phoenix has deserts and rocks. Despite their physical differences, both cities share a distinction. They are two of the world's hottest new tech cities. The roots behind their success are similar. Both Austin and Phoenix have universities and an attractive lifestyle.

Universities in both cities have aided high-tech industries. In Austin, the University of Texas was home to Michael Dell. Dell launched Dell, Inc. from his college dorm room. He set up his worldwide headquarters in Austin. Other high-tech businesses followed. Samsung, Hewlett Packard, and Intel now operate in the area. University of Texas continues to educate the workforce. Similarly, in Phoenix, Arizona State University educates many professionals. Phoenix has a concentration of high-tech companies. They include Intel and Motorola.

An attractive, low-cost environment also lures companies and workers to the two cities. In Austin, rent and housing prices are low. Austinites can buy a new four-bedroom home for $200,000. In California, the same house would cost $1 million. Austin's commercial rents also fall far below California's. These numbers are important because southern California is now the capital of the high-tech industry. Locals enjoy outdoor nature and culture, too. Hills, wildflowers, lakes, and rivers attract tourists. Likewise, Phoenix has low rents and housing prices. Residents can buy the same new home in Phoenix for about $250,000. And local business owners pay lower commercial rents than nationwide. In addition, Phoenix is famous for its sunny, outdoor lifestyle.

Both Austin and Phoenix have doubled their population in the past 25 years. Business experts expect more growth in the future. Austin and Phoenix will continue to be two of the hottest tech cities.

Using Comparison and Contrast Expressions

Writers use a range of expressions to signal that two subjects are similar or different. Use these expressions in your writing to signal similarities or differences between two subjects:

Comparison Expressions

EXPRESSIONS	EXAMPLES
similarly	Austin attracts musicians. **Similarly**, Phoenix draws artists.
similar	Austin has warm weather. Phoenix has a **similar** climate.
similarity(ies)	Many **similarities** exist between the two places.
both	**Both** cities have universities.
the same	The two cities have **the same** population.
likewise	Housing prices in Austin are lower than the national average. **Likewise**, housing costs in Phoenix are low.

Contrast Expressions

EXPRESSIONS	EXAMPLES
differ	Phoenix and Boston **differ** in their climates.
different	The two cities also have **different** types of industry.
difference(s)	The two places have numerous **differences**.
in contrast	Phoenix is located in a desert. **In contrast**, Boston is near the ocean.
while	**While** Phoenix has low housing costs, Boston has high-priced housing.
on the other hand	Phoenix has a low cost of living. **On the other hand**, it's expensive to live in Boston.

The landscapes of Austin, Texas, and Phoenix, Arizona, look very <u>different</u>. Austin has rolling green hills and rivers. Phoenix has deserts and rocks. Despite their physical <u>differences,</u> <u>both</u> cities share a distinction.

For more connecting words, including comparison and contrast expressions, refer to page 156.

Practice

A. *Scan the model essay. There are eleven compare-contrast expressions. Underline them. Circle any expressions that occur more than once. Discuss your answers in pairs.*

B. *Use the expressions in parentheses to show similarities between the two subjects. Make changes if necessary.*

1. The Austin area population doubled from 600,000 to over 1.2 million from 1980 to 2005. Phoenix's population rose from 1.5 million to more than 3.5 million in the same period. (likewise)

   The Austin area population doubled from 600,000 to over 1.2 million from 1980 to 2005. Likewise, Phoenix's population rose from 1.5 million to more than 3.5 million in the same period.

2. Austin attracts nature lovers. Phoenix attracts nature lovers. (both)

   _____

   _____

3. In Austin, new homes average $200,000. In Phoenix, new homes average $250,000. (similarly)

   _____

   _____

4. Austin has a hot climate. Phoenix has a hot climate. (the same)

   _____

   _____

5. Texas has natural landscapes. Arizona has natural landscapes. (similar)

   _____

   _____

C. Use the expressions in parentheses to show differences between the two subjects. Make changes if necessary.

1. Intel has a large design center in Austin. It has an even larger manufacturing center in Phoenix. (while)

   While Intel has a large design center in Austin, it has an even larger manufacturing center in Phoenix.

2. Austin has rolling hills. Phoenix has desert landscapes. (in contrast)

   _____

   _____

3. The summers in Phoenix are often unbearably hot. Summers in Boston are usually mild. (while)

   _____

   _____

4. Boston has a declining population rate. Population in Phoenix is rising. (on the other hand)

   _____

   _____

5. Boston has a well-developed public transit system. Phoenix has a limited public transit system. (differ)

   _____

   _____

WRITING ASSIGNMENT

Write an essay on the topic that you chose in Chapter 13. Use your proposal and outline and follow the steps to complete your essay.

STEP 1   Get ideas.

A. Read over the thesis statement and proposal that you wrote in Chapter 13.

B. Make a chart like the one below to take notes for each body paragraph in your essay. Each body paragraph should focus on one point of comparison. Present information about that point for Subject A and Subject B.

Point of Comparison

POINT		NOTES
	Subject A	
	Subject B	

C. Discuss your ideas with a partner. Make sure that you present ideas about each point of comparison for both subjects.

STEP 2   **Organize your ideas.**

Use your ideas from Step 1 and make an outline for your essay. Follow the example outline on pages 145–146. Show your outline to your instructor before you write.

STEP 3   **Write a rough draft.**

Write your essay. Use your outline from Step 2. Include vocabulary from the chapter where possible.

STEP 4   **Revise your rough draft.**

Read your paragraph. Use the Writing Checklist to look for mistakes. Work alone or in pairs.

Writing Checklist

❑ Does your essay follow your proposal and outline?

❑ Did you start each body paragraph with a topic sentence to introduce the point of comparison?

❑ Did you include in each body paragraph some supporting ideas about the point of comparison for each subject?

❑ Did you use comparison and contrast expressions correctly?

❑ Did you use vocabulary from the chapter appropriately?

STEP 5   **Edit your writing.**

    A. Edit your essay. Correct any mistakes in capitalization, punctuation, spelling, or verb use.

    B. Exchange essays with a partner. Use the Corrections Symbols on page 191 to mark each other's work.

    EXAMPLE

CAPITALIZATION ERROR

P

Many high-tech firms have moved to phoenix.

STEP 6   **Write a final copy.**

Correct your mistakes. Copy your final essay and give it to your instructor.

UNIT EIGHT

Literature

15

Bliss (Part 1)

A young woman looks out onto her garden.

PRE-READING

Discussion

Discuss these questions in pairs or small groups.

1. Katherine Mansfield (1888–1923) was one of the greatest short story writers in the English language. She wrote a fictional story titled "Bliss" about a young woman who is blissful, or extremely happy. This character is pictured in the drawing above. What do you predict that the story will say about the woman's life?

2. Literature is fiction—stories about people and things that are imaginary. Which do you prefer to read, fiction (stories that are not real) or nonfiction (books and articles about real facts or events)? Explain.

3. Do you know a famous piece of literature? If so, describe it.

Vocabulary

Read the sentences. Match the boldfaced words with the definitions.

___c___ 1. The young woman felt **as if** she would burst with happiness.

_____ 2. It was **quite** cold in the room, but Bertha still felt perfectly happy.

_____ 3. Bertha felt like she had **swallowed** a piece of sunshine.

_____ 4. Bertha's baby smiled **charmingly**, and the mother was attracted by the look.

_____ 5. Bertha loved her baby. To her, the baby was beautiful and amusing—a real **jewel**.

_____ 6. Bertha met a new friend at her club. She liked the woman so much that she considered her **a real find**.

_____ 7. Bertha's new friend was quiet and beautiful. **Beyond** that, Bertha knew very little about her.

_____ 8. Miss Fulton had a strange smile, and Bertha felt there was something else **behind** it.

---

a. in a very pleasing or attractive manner
b. something or someone as precious as a small valuable stone
c. in a way that suggests that something is true; like
d. in addition to; more than
e. responsible for something or causing something to happen
f. make food or drink go down your throat
g. something very good or valuable that you discover by chance
h. very but not extremely

Bliss

By Katherine Mansfield

Part 1

1   Although Bertha Young was 30, she still sometimes wanted to run instead of walk. She wanted to dance in the street. She wanted to throw something up in the air and catch it again, or to stand still and laugh at—nothing—at nothing, simply.

2   What can you do if you are 30 and, suddenly, turning the corner of your own street, you feel perfectly happy, **as if** you had **swallowed** a piece of the late afternoon sun?

3   She ran up the steps of her house. It was **quite** dark and cold in the dining room. Bertha still threw off her coat, and the cold air fell on her arms.

4   But she still had that feeling of perfect happiness, as if she had swallowed a piece of sunshine. She did not want to breathe. The feeling might get stronger, but still she breathed, deeply, deeply. She did not want to look in the cold mirror, but still she did look, and saw a woman with smiling lips and big, dark eyes. She looked as if she was waiting for somebody, as if she was waiting for something to happen. Something must happen.

* * * *

5   Nurse sat at a low table giving little B her supper after her bath. The baby looked up when she saw her mother and began to jump.

6   "Now, my love, eat it up like a good girl," said Nurse.

7   Bertha knew that Nurse did not like her to come in at the wrong time.

Katherine Mansfield

8   "Has she been good, Nurse?"

9   "She's been a little sweet all afternoon," whispered Nurse. "We went to the park and a big dog came along. She pulled its ear. Oh, you should have seen her."

10   Bertha wanted to say that it was dangerous to pull a strange dog's ear, but she was rather afraid of Nurse. She stood watching them, her hands by her side, like the poor little girl in front of the rich little girl.

11   The baby looked up at her again, and then smiled so **charmingly** that Bertha cried: "Oh, Nurse, please let me finish giving her supper while you put the bath things away."

12   Nurse went out of the room with the bath towels.

13   "Now I've got you to myself, my little **jewel**," said Bertha.

14   When the soup was finished, Bertha turned round to the fire.

15   "You're nice—you're very nice!" she said, kissing her warm baby. Again, she felt perfectly happy.

16   "You're wanted on the telephone," said Nurse, as she took the baby from Bertha.

    * * * *

17   She ran downstairs and picked up the telephone. It was Harry.

18   "Oh, is that you, Ber? Look here. I'll be late. I'll take a taxi and come along as quickly as I can, but can we have dinner ten minutes later? All right?"

19   "Yes, perfectly all right. Oh, Harry!"

20   "Yes?"

21   What did she want to say? She had nothing to say. She only wanted to tell him what she was feeling. It would be silly to say: "Hasn't it been a wonderful day?"

22   "What is it?" asked the voice on the telephone.

23   "Nothing," said Bertha.

    * * * *

24   There were people coming to dinner. Mr. and Mrs. Norman Knight were an interesting couple. He was going to start a theater, and she was interested in furniture. There was a young man, Eddie Warren, who had just written a little book of poems. And there was a "find" of Bertha's, a young woman called Pearl Fulton. Bertha did not know what Miss Fulton did. They had met at the club and Bertha had liked her immediately. She always liked beautiful women who had something strange about them.

25   Bertha and Miss Fulton had met a number of times, and they had talked together a lot, but Bertha could still not understand her friend. Miss Fulton told Bertha everything about some parts of her life, but beyond that she told her nothing.

26   Was there anything beyond it? Harry said "No." He thought Miss Fulton was boring, and "cold, like all fair-haired women, and perhaps not very intelligent." But Bertha did not agree with him.

27   "No, the way she has of sitting with her head a little on one side, and smiling, has something behind it, Harry, and I must find out what it is."

28   She went into the sitting room and lighted the fire and rearranged the furniture a little. The room came alive at once.

29   "I'm too happy—too happy!" she said to herself. Really—really—she had everything. She was young. Harry and she were as much in love as ever, and they were really good friends. She had a lovely baby. They didn't have to worry about money. They had a wonderful house and garden. And friends—modern, exciting friends, writers and painters and people who wrote poems—just the kind of friends they wanted.

30   She sat up. She felt weak with happiness. It must be the spring.

Identifying Main Ideas

Read each question. Circle the letter of the best answer.

1. What is the writer's main point about Bertha Young?
    a. She had a baby.
    b. She had a nice home.
    c. She was married.
    d. She was very happy.

2. What did Bertha do when she visited her baby?
   a. She fed the baby her supper.
   b. She gave the baby a bath.
   c. She watched Nurse dress the baby.
   d. She took the baby to the park.

3. Why did Bertha's husband, Harry, call her?
   a. To say that they were having dinner guests.
   b. To say that he would be late to dinner.
   c. To say that he was perfectly happy.
   d. To say that it was a wonderful day.

4. What did Bertha know about her friend, Miss Fulton?
   a. Bertha understood her completely.
   b. She did not understand her friend.
   c. She knew all about her friend's life.
   d. She knew that her friend was intelligent.

Identifying Details

Each statement below is incorrect. Look at the reading again and correct the statement.

1. Bertha Young was ~~20~~ *30* years old.

2. Bertha had small, light-colored eyes.

3. While Bertha was out, her husband Harry cared for the baby.

4. That night, Bertha and Harry were having six guests to dinner.

5. Bertha thought Miss Fulton was boring and not very intelligent.

Making Inferences

What meaning can be inferred from the passage? Circle the letter of the best answer.

1. What can you do if you are 30 and, suddenly, turning the corner of your own street, you feel perfectly happy, as if you had swallowed a piece of the late afternoon sun?
   a. Bertha was surprised by her happy feeling.
   b. Bertha had this happy feeling all the time.

2. Bertha wanted to say that it was dangerous to pull a strange dog's ear, but she was rather afraid of Nurse. She stood watching them, her hands by her side, like the poor little girl in front of the rich little girl.

   a. Bertha was the baby's main caregiver.

   b. Bertha was not the baby's main caregiver.

3. What did she want to say? She had nothing to say. She only wanted to tell him what she was feeling. It would be silly to say: "Hasn't it been a wonderful day?"

   a. Bertha is embarrassed to say that she is feeling happy.

   b. Bertha is afraid to say that she is feeling happy.

4. Miss Fulton told Bertha everything about some parts of her life, but beyond that she told her nothing. ". . . the way she has of sitting with her head a little on one side, and smiling, has something behind it, Harry, and I must find out what it is."

   a. Bertha is curious to learn more about her friend.

   b. Bertha is afraid of learning about her friend.

READING SKILL

Using Literary Terms

Reading literature differs from reading nonfiction texts. When you discuss or write about literature, use these terms:

- **Characters:** The people in a story are called the characters.
- **Setting:** The setting is the time and place in which the story takes place. Sometimes the exact or approximate time and place are stated. Other times, the reader must guess the time and place.
- **Plot:** The plot is the series of related events in a story.

Practice

A. Answer the questions. Discuss your answers in pairs or small groups.

1. Who are the main characters in Katherine Mansfield's short story, "Bliss"? Write a description for each character.

   a. Bertha Young: _____

   b. Little "B": _____

   c. Nurse: _____

   d. Harry Young: _____

   e. Miss Fulton: _____

   f. Mr. and Mrs. Knight: _____

   g. Eddie Warren: _____

2. Mansfield (1888–1923) lived in New Zealand and England. What can you guess about the setting of the story? Write your guesses below.

a. Time: _____

b. Place: _____

B. The sentences describing the plot are not in order. Number them in the correct order.

_____ Harry thinks that Miss Fulton is unintelligent.

_____ Bertha visits her baby and feeds her.

_____ Bertha arrives home, feeling happy.

_____ Bertha's husband, Harry, calls her on the phone.

_____ She remembers that she will be having guests.

_____ Bertha thinks of all the things that she has in her life.

_____ Bertha thinks about her new friend, Miss Fulton.

FROM READING TO WRITING

Journal
Choose one question and write a journal entry.

Reflecting on the Reading

Discuss the questions in pairs or small groups.

1. In the story, "Bliss," the young woman felt "perfectly happy." What does it mean to feel "perfect" happiness?
2. Do you think that Bertha had good reasons to be so happy? Explain.

Vocabulary
For more practice with vocabulary, go to page 206.

Activating Your Vocabulary

Take notes on these questions. Try to use your answers in your Writing Assignment.

1. Have you ever felt **as if** you had **swallowed** a piece of the sun? Explain.
2. Do you know a person who acts **charmingly**? Describe how this person acts.
3. Is there someone that you consider a **jewel**? Why do you feel this way?
4. Do you know someone who is **quite** intelligent? How does that person display his or her intelligence?
5. What feelings are sometimes **behind** a person's smile?

Read the model paragraph.

MODEL

Little Bertha, the Baby

In her short story, "Bliss," Katherine Mansfield describes the baby as a sweet child. In the first part of the story, Little B, the baby, smiles when her mother enters the room. This charming behavior gets her mother's attention, and soon, her mother wants to feed her and be alone with her. The baby also behaves well with her nurse. The nurse even tells Bertha what "a little sweet" the baby has been that day. She tells the mother how the baby played with a dog in a park. All in all, the baby appears to be a sweet and loving child.

WRITING SKILL

Writing a Character Analysis

To *analyze* means to examine or think about something carefully in order to understand it. A **character analysis** examines and draws conclusions about a character in a literary work. When you write a character analysis, you give your opinion about the personality and motivations of a character, using examples from the story to support your opinion.

To write a one-paragraph character analysis, follow these steps.

- **Choose a character.** It should be one that you have strong feelings about.
- **Choose a word or words that best describe the character's personality.** Write a sentence with the character's name and his or her main quality. This will be the topic sentence of your paragraph.

  EXAMPLE

  In her short story, "Bliss," Katherine Mansfield describes the baby as a sweet child.

- **Find at least two examples to show that the character has the quality you chose.** Use the character's words, actions, or appearance. Present these ideas in direct quotations from the story or in paraphrases (restatements in your words). Summarize important events relating to the character's quality. Assume that the reader does not know the story. Do not tell the entire plot of the story.
- **Explain each idea.** Include at least one sentence from the story. In your words, explain how or why the character's words, actions, or appearance show that he or she has the quality you are writing about.

- **Add a concluding sentence.** It should restate your topic sentence.
- **Be consistent with verbs.** Use the present tense to write your character analysis.

EXAMPLE

> In the first part of the story, Little B, the baby, **smiles** when her mother **enters** the room.

Practice

Skim the model paragraph to answer these questions. Work in pairs.

1. What quality does the writer believe that the character has?
2. Write the numbers *1* and *2* above the sentences that present the first and second supporting ideas from the story. Do the supporting ideas from the story represent the character's words, actions, and/or appearance?
3. Underline sentences that explain supporting ideas 1 and 2.
4. Do these sentences include words that tell the reader about the plot of the story?
5. Does the paragraph have a conclusion? If so, circle that sentence.

Using Appositives

An **appositive** is a noun phrase that renames and describes another noun. Use appositives when you write about a character in a story. Follow these guidelines for writing an appositive:

- **Begin with the ideas in two simple sentences.**

EXAMPLE

> Little B is the baby. Little B smiles when her mother enters the room.

- **Combine the sentences into one sentence with one verb. Set the appositive off from the rest of the sentence with commas.**

EXAMPLE

> ┌ APPOSITIVE ┐
> Little B, **the baby,** smiles when her mother enters the room.

Practice

Combine each pair of sentences into one sentence, using an appositive.

1. Bertha Young ~~was~~ a 30-year-old married woman. ~~She~~ made a new friend.

Bertha Young, a 30-year-old married woman, made a new friend.

2. Her friend was Pearl Fulton. Pearl Fulton had a secretive smile.

   _____

3. Bertha's garden was a beautiful space. The garden had a pear tree.

   _____

4. Harry Young was Bertha's husband. Harry enjoyed good food.

   _____

5. Eddie Warren was a young poet. Eddie was one of Harry's friends.

   _____

6. Mr. and Mrs. Knight were a married couple. They were also friends of Harry and Bertha.

   _____

WRITING ASSIGNMENT

Write a one-paragraph character analysis about the story "Bliss." Follow the steps.

STEP 1 **Get ideas.**

A. The chart below lists each character and one word to describe him or her. Add other words to describe each character.

CHARACTER	QUALITIES
Bertha Young	happy
Nurse	hard-working
The baby	sweet
Harry Young	busy
Miss Fulton	strange

B. Discuss the characters in pairs. Then choose the character and qualities that you will include in your writing.

C. Find two ideas from the story to support the person's qualities. Add the heading *Support* to your chart to take notes about those ideas. Include the following:

- Direct quotations or a paraphrase (restatement) of information from the story
- Sentence(s) to explain how this idea shows the character has these qualities
- A brief summary of the important events occurring at this place in the story (not the entire plot of the story)

D. Explain your notes to a partner. Add supporting details to your notes. Choose ideas from your notes to include in your writing.

STEP 2   Organize your ideas.

Make an outline to organize your paragraph.

I. **Topic sentence** Include the character's name and identification and the quality that you will write about.

   A. **Support 1:** Present the first piece of support from the story. Include words that tell the events that are occurring in this place in the story. Add at least one sentence to explain how the supporting idea shows the character has this quality.

   B. **Support 2:** Present the second piece of support from the story. Include the same kinds of ideas that you did for support 1.

II. **Conclusion** Add a concluding sentence to restate your topic sentence.

STEP 3   Write a rough draft.

Write your paragraph. Include vocabulary from the chapter where possible.

STEP 4   Revise your rough draft.

Read your paragraph. Use the Writing Checklist to look for mistakes. Work alone or in pairs.

Writing Checklist

❑ Does your paragraph have a topic sentence that states the character's name and his or her qualities?

❑ Does your paragraph include at least two ideas from the story that show that the character has this quality?

❑ Does your paragraph include at least one sentence of explanation (to show that the idea from the story supports the topic sentence)?

❑ Does your paragraph include sentences to explain the events that are occurring at this place in the story?

❑ Did you use appositives correctly?

❑ Did you use vocabulary from the chapter appropriately?

STEP 5 **Edit your writing.**

A. Edit your paragraph. Correct any mistakes in capitalization, punctuation, spelling, or verb use.

B. Exchange paragraphs with a partner. Use the Correction Symbols on page 191 to mark each other's work.

EXAMPLE

VERB TENSE ERROR (v.t.)

smiles

The baby ~~smiled~~ when her mother looks at her.

STEP 6 **Write a final copy.**

Correct your mistakes. Copy your final paragraph and give it to your instructor.

Bliss (Part 2)

*In this chapter
you will:*

• read the end of
the short story
about a happy
young woman

• use support
from a reading
in your writing

• write a character
analysis essay

Bertha and her friend at the dinner party

PRE-READING

Discussion

Discuss the questions in pairs or small groups.

1. What do you think will happen to Bertha Young? How will the
   story of this young woman end?
2. Does her story interest you? Why or why not?
3. Does the story remind you of anything about your own life or the
   life of someone you know? Explain.

Vocabulary

Circle the letter of the word or phrase that is NOT close in meaning to the boldfaced word.

1. Harry lived life with **enthusiasm**. He enjoyed keeping busy and spending time with friends.
   a. eagerness   b. boredom   c. interest

2. However, Harry spoke **coolly** about the young woman. He seemed to take no interest in her.
   a. in a slightly unfriendly way   b. unexcitedly   c. warmly

3. Bertha thought her dinner guests were **delightful**. She liked being with them.
   a. amusing   b. disagreeable   c. pleasant

4. The guests were **pleased** by the dinner. Both the food and the atmosphere were good.
   a. discontented   b. satisfied   c. happy

5. The two women stood **side by side** in front of the windows, looking at the garden.
   a. together   b. next to each other   c. in front of each other

6. Eddie Warren **disliked** riding in taxis by himself. It made him nervous.
   a. was fond of   b. hated   c. had an objection to

7. Harry showed **rudeness** toward Miss Fulton by his looks and actions.
   a. honor   b. lack of respect   c. impoliteness

8. The tall pear tree was the most **lovely** part of Bertha's garden.
   a. peaceful   b. beautiful   c. unattractive

Bliss

By Katherine Mansfield

Part 2

1   The bell rang. It was Eddie Warren. He knew the Norman Knights.

2   Harry shouted: "Hello, you people. Down in five minutes." Bertha smiled. She liked his **enthusiasm**. To other people he sometimes seemed strange, but they did not know him well. She understood him. She talked and laughed until Harry came down. She had forgotten that Pearl Fulton had not arrived.

3   "I wonder if Miss Fulton has forgotten?"

4   "Probably," said Harry.

5   "Ah! There's a taxi now." Bertha smiled when she thought about her new friend. "She lives in taxis."

6   "She'll get fat if she does," said Harry **coolly**.

7   "Harry—don't," warned Bertha, laughing at him.

8   They waited, and then Miss Fulton came in. She was all in silver, and she smiled with her head a little to the side.

9   "Am I late?"

10   "No, not at all," said Bertha. "Come along." And she took Miss Fulton's arm, and they moved into the dining room. The touch of that cool arm gave Bertha that same perfectly happy feeling again.

11   Miss Fulton did not look at her, but then she rarely looked straight at people. Her heavy eyelids lay upon her eyes, and the strange half-smile came and went on her lips. She seemed to live by listening more than seeing. But Bertha felt as if they were very close, as if they understood each other very well.

12   She and Miss Fulton were closer, Bertha felt, than the other guests, as they all ate dinner and talked together. They were all dears, and she loved having them there at her table. She loved giving them wonderful food. In fact, she wanted to tell them how **delightful** they were, how nice they looked.

13   Harry was enjoying his dinner. Bertha was **pleased** when he turned to her and said: "Bertha, this is wonderful."

14   She felt as if she loved the whole world. Everything was good—was right.

* * * *

15   At last, the meal was over.

16   "Do you have a garden?" said the cool, sleepy voice of Miss Fulton.

17   Bertha crossed the room, pulled the curtains back, and opened those long windows.

18   And the two women stood **side by side**, looking at the flowering pear tree. How long did they stand there? They understood each other perfectly. They were in a circle of light; they were like people from another world.

* * * *

19   Miss Fulton sat in the lowest, deepest chair and Harry offered cigarettes.

20   From the way he offered Miss Fulton the cigarette box, Bertha could see that Miss Fulton not only bored Harry; he really **disliked** her. And she decided that Miss Fulton felt this, too, and was hurt.

21   "Oh, Harry, don't dislike her," Bertha said to herself. "You are quite wrong about her. She's wonderful. And besides, how can you feel so differently about someone who means so much to me?"

22   At those last words, Bertha suddenly thought: "Soon these people will go. The house will be quiet. The lights will be out. And you and he will be alone together."

23   For the first time in her life, Bertha Young wanted her husband.

24   Oh, she had been in love with him, of course. But her feelings were different from his. They talked together about it—they were such good friends.

25   But now she felt different. She really wanted him. Was this the meaning of that feeling of perfect happiness?

26   "My dear," said Mrs. Knight to Bertha, "we mustn't miss our train. It's been so nice."

27   "I'll come with you to the door," said Bertha. "I loved having you."

28   When she got back into the sitting room, the others were getting ready to leave.

29   Miss Fulton moved towards the door, and Bertha was following when Harry almost pushed past.

30   "Let me help you."

31   Bertha knew that Harry was feeling sorry for his **rudeness** to Miss Fulton, so she let him go.

32   Eddie and she stood by the fire.

33   She turned her head towards the hall. And she saw . . . Harry with Miss Fulton's coat in his arms and Miss Fulton with her back turned to him and her head bent. Harry threw the coat down, put his hands on her shoulders, and turned her to him. His lips said: "I love you," and Miss Fulton laid her white fingers on his cheeks and smiled her sleepy smile. Harry smiled, too, and he whispered: "Tomorrow," and with her eyelids Miss Fulton said: "Yes."

34   "If you prefer," said Harry's voice, very loud, from outside, "I can phone for a taxi."

35   "Oh, no. It's not necessary," said Miss Fulton, and she came up to Bertha and gave her the thin white fingers to hold.

36   "Good-bye. Thank you so much."

37   "Good-bye," said Bertha.

38   Miss Fulton held her hand a moment longer.

39   And then she was gone, with Eddie following.

40   "I'll lock the doors," said Harry, very calmly.

41   Bertha ran to the long windows.

42   "Oh, what is going to happen now?" she cried.

43   But the pear tree was as **lovely** as ever and as full of flowers as before.

Identifying Main Ideas

Put the plot of Part 2 of the story in the correct order. Write the numbers 1–7.

____ Harry acts bored by Miss Fulton.

____ Bertha tells the Knights good-bye, and they leave.

____ Harry holds Miss Fulton and says he loves her.

____ Harry compliments Bertha on the wonderful meal.

____ The guests arrive at Bertha's home for dinner.

____ Bertha looks out at the garden and wonders what will happen.

____ Bertha and Miss Fulton stand together and look at the garden.

Identifying Details

Match the quotes to the correct speaker and the listener in the story. Complete the sentences below each quote.

1. "Am I late?"

   _____ said this to _____.

2. "Bertha, this is wonderful."

   _____ said this to _____.

3. "How can you feel so differently about someone who means so much to me?"

   _____ thought this about _____.

4. "Do you have a garden?"

   _____ said this to _____.

5. "We mustn't miss our train. It's been so nice."

   _____ said this to _____.

Making Inferences

What meaning can be inferred from the passage? Circle the letter of the best answer.

1. The two women stood side by side, looking at the flowering pear tree. How long did they stand there? They understood each other perfectly. They were in a circle of light; they were like people from another world.

   a. The two women seemed closer than the others in the group.

   b. The two women did not like being with the others in the group.

2. For the first time in her life, Bertha Young wanted her husband. Oh, she had been in love with him, of course. But her feelings were different from his. They talked together about it—they were such good friends.

   a. Bertha often showed her husband that she wanted to be with him.

   b. Bertha rarely showed her husband that she wanted to be with him.

3. His lips said: "I love you," and Miss Fulton laid her white fingers on his cheeks and smiled her sleepy smile. Harry smiled, too, and he whispered: "Tomorrow," and with her eyelids Miss Fulton said: "Yes."

   a. Harry and Miss Fulton had been seeing each other secretly before this evening.

   b. Harry and Miss Fulton would see each other secretly for the first time the next day.

4. But the pear tree was as lovely as ever and as full of flowers as before.

    a. The garden was the same though so much had just changed.

    b. The garden was the same because nothing else had changed.

FROM READING TO WRITING

Journal
Choose one question and write a journal entry.

Reflecting on the Reading

Discuss the questions in pairs or small groups.

1. What is your reaction to Harry's behavior at the end of the story? What kind of husband do you think he is?
2. What is your reaction to Miss Fulton? What kind of friend do you think she is?
3. What will Bertha do in the future? What should she do?

Vocabulary
For more practice with vocabulary, go to page 207.

Activating Your Vocabulary

Take notes on these questions. Try to use your answers in your Writing Assignment.

1. Which of the characters in the story do you have the greatest **enthusiasm** for? Explain.
2. Do you like people who act **coolly** toward others? Why or why not?
3. This **delightful** evening had a disastrous end for Bertha. Explain.
4. Were you **pleased** by any of the characters in the story? Why or why not?
5. Did you **dislike** any of the characters in the story? Why or why not?

WRITING

WRITING SKILL

Organizing a Character Analysis Essay

Use the following outline to organize your character analysis essay.

I. **Introduction:** Begin with a sentence that includes the author and title of the work and briefly summarizes what the story is about. End this paragraph with a thesis statement with the character's name and identification. Include two qualities that you will write about.

    EXAMPLE

    Miss Fulton was a mysterious and sensual woman.

II. **Body Paragraph 1—Quality 1:** Include a topic sentence to present the first quality of the character.

   A. *Support 1*

      1. Describe the character's action, words, or appearance—to show that he or she has the quality. Include words that tell the events that are occurring in this place in the story.

      2. Add at least one sentence to explain how the supporting idea shows the character has this quality.

   B. *Support 2:* Present the second piece of support from the reading. Include the same kinds of ideas that you did for support 1.

III. **Body Paragraph 2—Quality 2:** Include a topic sentence to present the second quality of the character.

   A. Support 1: Present the first piece of support from the reading to support quality 2. Include the same kinds of ideas that you did for support 1 in body paragraph 1.

   B. Support 2: Present the second piece of support from the reading. Include the same kinds of ideas that you did for support 1 in body paragraph 1.

IV. **Conclusion:** Restate the thesis statement. Close the essay by summarizing your main points and/or adding another piece of support from the text that restates your opinion.

   EXAMPLE

   She behaved secretively and sensually throughout the story.

Practice

Read this character analysis. Then answer the questions. Discuss your answers in pairs.

Laura and "The Garden Party"

Laura Sheridan, a daughter in Katherine Mansfield's "The Garden Party," is the main character in the story about a rich family's garden party. Everyone in the Sheridan family seems similar. Only Laura stands out. This young woman attracts the reader's attention by her sensitive but immature personality.

From the start, Laura shows her sensitivity. She is supposed to be in charge of planning the family party. When she learns that a neighbor has died, she decides to cancel the party. "We can't possibly have a garden party with a man dead just outside the gate," Laura tells her sister. Laura is sensitive. She knows that the party will have music and fun, and she feels this is inappropriate because of the man's death. But her mother says that she must be sensible. No one agrees with Laura's request to stop the party.

Later, Laura shows that she is more immature than sensitive. When her mother tells her that the party will go on, she gives Laura a new hat so that she will feel better. Laura takes the hat and puts it on. The girl looks at herself in the mirror and soon forgets that a man has died. She is very immature. She is more concerned with her new clothing than a person's death.

At the end of the story, however, Laura again shows her sensitivity. Her mother suggests that Laura take food to the dead man's family. When she sees the man's widow and his dead body, she cries and runs from their home. By these actions, the young girl shows that she is both sensitive and immature.

1. Circle the thesis statement of the essay. Underline the two qualities that the writer describes about the character.
2. Reread the paragraph about the first quality. Underline the topic sentence. Which supporting sentences include information from the reading? Which sentence(s) explain(s) the meaning of those sentences?
3. Underline the topic sentence in the paragraph about the second quality. Which supporting sentences include information from the reading? Which sentence(s) explain(s) the meaning of those sentences?
4. In the conclusion, underline the sentence that restates the thesis.

WRITING SKILL

Using Support from a Reading

You can use information from a reading to **support ideas** in your writing. Do this by quoting the information directly from the reading or by paraphrasing the information.

Direct Quotations

Use a direct quotation from a reading when the original language is effective and you do not want to restate the idea in your own words. A quotation from a reading should be included within a sentence. Here are two common methods for doing this:

- **Include a complete quotation.**

    EXAMPLE

    "We can't possibly have a garden party with a man dead just outside the gate," Laura tells her sister.

- **Include part of a quotation as part of your sentence.**

    EXAMPLE

    > The nurse even tells Bertha what "a little sweet" the baby has been that day.

    Be sure to use correct punctuation with quotations.

Paraphrasing

When you paraphrase, you present someone else's ideas in your own words. Follow these guidelines for paraphrasing:

- **Identify the source of the information.** Put the name of a story in quotation marks, and underline the name of a book.

    EXAMPLE

    > In her short story, "Bliss," Katherine Mansfield describes the baby as a sweet child.

- **Use your own words.** Do not use more than two words together exactly from the original text. Restate the author's ideas in a new way.
- **Keep the meaning of the original text.**

    EXAMPLE

    > She tells the mother how the baby played with a dog in a park.

- **Do not include your opinion.**

Practice

Read paragraphs 23 to 25 again of "Bliss," Part 2. Choose the best paraphrase for the passage. Discuss your answer in pairs.

Paraphrase 1   During the party, Bertha Young thinks about her husband. For once, she wants to be alone with him. She admits that she once loved him, but says that they were friends. Now her feelings have changed, and she wants him.

Paraphrase 2   At this point in the party, Bertha is dreaming of her husband. For the first time in her life, Bertha Young wants her husband. She remembers that she had been in love with him, of course. But her feelings are different from his. They were such good friends. But now she feels different. She really wants him.

Paraphrase 3   Bertha thinks she would like to be alone with her husband. She stopped loving him, but for some reason, she changes her mind. It seems like this woman does not know what she wants. She needs to decide if she loves her husband or not, and tell him. Then she can be truly happy.

WRITING ASSIGNMENT

Write a character analysis of the character that you wrote about in Chapter 15. Follow the steps.

STEP 1 **Get ideas.**

A. Read over the paragraph that you wrote in Chapter 15. You will use this paragraph as one of the body paragraphs in your essay.

B. Brainstorm a second quality about your character. Review the chart on page 171, and choose another word to describe the character's personality. Share your idea in pairs.

C. As you did in Chapter 15, find two ideas from the story to support your opinion that the character has this quality. Take notes about the ideas. Include the following:

- Direct quotations or a paraphrase (restatement) of information from the story
- Sentence(s) to explain how this idea shows the character has these qualities
- A brief description of the events occurring at this place in the story (not the entire plot of the story)

D. Work in pairs. Explain your notes and revise them if necessary. Choose ideas from your notes to include in your writing.

STEP 2 **Organize your ideas.**

A. Write a thesis statement for your essay. Include the character's name and the two qualities that you believe he or she has.

EXAMPLES

This young woman attracts the reader's attention by her sensitive but immature personality.

Miss Fulton was a mysterious and sensual woman.

B. Make an outline for your essay. Follow the outline on pages 179–180. Show your outline to your instructor before you write.

STEP 3 **Write a rough draft.**

Write your essay. Use the outline from Step 2. Include vocabulary from the chapter where possible.

Revise your rough draft.

Read your essay. Use the Writing Checklist to look for mistakes. Work alone or in pairs.

Writing Checklist

❑ Does your introduction include the author and title of the work and a brief summary of the story?

❑ Does the introduction end with a thesis statement that states the character's name and his or her two qualities?

❑ Does each body paragraph begin with a topic sentence that presents one quality? Does the paragraph include two supporting points?

❑ Did you use direct quotations or paraphrasing appropriately?

❑ Did you explain how the information from the story supports your main ideas?

❑ Did you use vocabulary from the chapter appropriately?

STEP 5 **Edit your writing.**

A. Edit your essay. Correct any mistakes in capitalization, punctuation, spelling, or verb use.

B. Exchange essays with a partner. Use the Correction Sybmols on page 191 to mark each other's work.

EXAMPLE

VERB TENSE ERROR (v.t.)
looked
Harry ~~looks~~ bored when Pearl Fulton talked.

STEP 6 **Write a final copy.**

Correct your mistakes. Copy your final essay and give it to your instructor.

Avoiding Plagiarism

Plagiarism means to pass off someone else's words or ideas as your own. In other words, it means stealing someone else's work. It happens when you use an author's ideas or copy an author's words in a paper, but you do not include his or her name. You can avoid plagiarizing the words or ideas of an author by *quoting* or *paraphrasing*.

Quoting

Quoting means using the exact same phrases or sentences from a piece of writing. To signal these words are quoted, put quotation marks " " around them. If the quote does not start the sentence, put a comma before the first quotation mark. Always place the concluding period or question mark inside the second quotation mark.

EXAMPLE

> According to Davies, "The right to privacy is the right to protect ourselves against intrusion from the outside world."

Below are a few different ways to introduce a quote. Be sure to always include the author's last name.

- **According to** Davies, ".."
- Davies **says**, ".."
- Davies **states**, ".."

Paraphrasing

Paraphrasing means taking one or more sentences from a reading, and writing the same ideas, but in your own words. Here are a few general rules to follow when paraphrasing.

- Include the author's last name.

- Make your paraphrase about the same length as the original quote.

- Make sure that your paraphrase sounds different from the original.

- Don't change the meaning in the original quote. *Same idea, different words.*

Here are some ways to state the same idea using different words:

- Change the words and wording as much as possible by using synonyms.

- Use different forms of the same word (adjective, noun, verb, adverb).

- Try to put the ideas from the quote in a different order in your paraphrase.

Read the following quote. Compare the quote to the incorrect and correct paraphrases.

QUOTE

"The widespread adoption of tracking won't be done against our will but initially with our consent," says Davies.

INCORRECT PARAPHRASE

According to Davies, the widespread use of tracking won't be done against our wishes but with our approval.

CORRECT PARAPHRASE

According to Davies, people won't object to the use of tracking when it becomes prevalent; in the beginning, people will accept it.

The first paraphrase is incorrect because it is too similar to the original quote. Many words are repeated, so the sentence sounds almost the same as the original. In the correct paraphrase, the sentences sound very different, but the idea has remained the same. The correct paraphrase uses synonyms and different wording to state the same idea. This chart shows the original words and how they were replaced in the paraphrase.

ORIGINAL WORDING	PARAPHRASE
widespread	prevalent
the adoption of tracking	the use of tracking
won't be done against our will	people won't object to
initially	in the beginning
with our consent	people will accept it

Practice

Circle the letter of the best paraphrase for each quote.

1. According to Davies, "The right to privacy is the right to protect ourselves against intrusion from the outside world."

   a. According to Davies, the right to privacy is the right to defend ourselves against intrusions from the outside.

   b. According to Davies, the right to protect ourselves against intrusion from the world is the right to privacy.

   c. According to Davies, everyone has the right to stop the outside world from invading his or her privacy.

2. Levy believes that "sooner or later . . . we will realize that information taken from our movements has compromised our 'locational privacy.'"

   a. Sooner or later, people will figure out that information taken from their movements has compromised their "locational privacy," according to Levy.

   b. People will eventually see that their "locational privacy" has been threatened by the collection of data about their movements, according to Levy.

   c. According to Levy, we will realize that information taken from our movements has compromised our "locational privacy"— sooner or later.

3. "In a majority of countries, employers are permitted—'within reason'—to place all employees under constant surveillance," says Davies.

   a. Within reason, employers are permitted to place all workers under constant surveillance in a majority of countries, says Davies.

   b. Businesses are allowed to keep track of their workers in most countries around the world, says Davies.

   c. In a majority of countries, employers are allowed to put all their employees under constant surveillance, says Davies.

Grammar Reference

SENTENCE TYPES

Simple Sentences

TYPE 1 With one subject and one verb

S + V   Sam works.

TYPE 2 With more than one subject and a verb

S + S + V   Sam and Helen work.

TYPE 3 With one subject and more than one verb

S + V + V   Sam works and plays.

TYPE 4 With more than one subject and more than one verb

S + S + V + V   Sam and Helen work and play.

Compound Sentences

TYPE 1 With a comma and a coordinating conjunction

S + V { , and / , but / , for / , nor / , or / , so / , yet } **S + V**   Sam works, but Helen plays.

TYPE 2 With a semicolon

S + V   ;   **S + V**   Sam works; Helen plays.

TYPE 3 With a semicolon and a transition followed by a comma

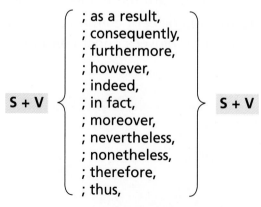

S + V { ; as a result, / ; consequently, / ; furthermore, / ; however, / ; indeed, / ; in fact, / ; moreover, / ; nevertheless, / ; nonetheless, / ; therefore, / ; thus, } **S + V**

Complex Sentences

TYPE 1 With a subordinating conjunction midsentence

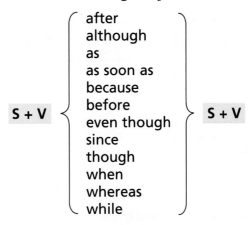

TYPE 2 With an initial subordinating conjunction (often with a comma after the initial clause)

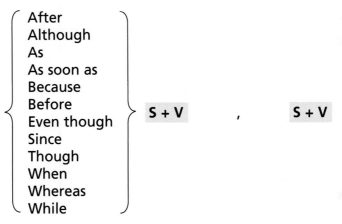

	TRANSITION SIGNALS	COORDINATING CONJUNCTIONS	SUBORDINATING CONJUNCTIONS
To give an **additional idea**	also, in addition, moreover,	, and	—
To show **direct contrast**	however, in contrast, on the other hand,	, but	while whereas
To show **unexpected contrast**	nevertheless, nonetheless,	, yet	although even though though
To show **cause**	—	, for	because since
To show **effect**	as a result, consequently, for this reason, therefore, thus,	, so	—
To show **similarity**	in addition, likewise, similarly	, and	—
To show **time relationships**	after that, before that, later, then	—	before after when while as as soon as since

Correction Symbols

SYMBOL	MEANING	EXAMPLE
a/p	active/passive error	*a/p* The house **located** on a busy street.
art	wrong article or missing article	*art* I read **book** yesterday.
agr	subject-verb agreement error	*agr* Mr. Schmidt **listen** to music in his car.
E	not an English word	*E* Anna wanted to go to school, **pero** she was sick.
nn	not necessary	*nn* My professor lives in **the** Chicago.
P	punctuation error	*P* You're right, I should study harder.
s	subject missing	*s* **Is** not easy to speak in English on the telephone.
sp.	spelling error	*sp.* This is an **exampul** of a spelling error.
s/p	singular/plural error	*s/p* There are many **student** in my class.
v	verb missing	*v* **I from** China.
v.t.	verb tense error	*v.t.* I **drive** my car to work last night.
wf	wrong form of word	*wf* He always walks very **quick**.
pp	wrong preposition or missing preposition	*pp* The children should not play **on** the house.
ww	wrong word	*ww* She **said** me to go home.
/	lower-case	We went to the P̸ark on a sunny D̸ay.
≡	upper-case	my classes end on may 15.
◯	missing word	My mother needs to **go** ◯ **the** doctor.
∿	reverse word order	I enjoy spending time with my (**friends** **good**.)

Vocabulary Review

Chapter 1

A *Read each sentence. Write a word from the box above the boldfaced word or phrase with the same meaning.*

~~alter~~	contributes to	researchers
artificial	function	stress
consider	makes sense	

1. When Paul started working at night, he had to **change** (*alter*) his sleep
   schedule. Now, he sleeps in the day.

2. What do you **think of as** "enough sleep"? Is it six hours, eight
   hours, ten hours, or some other amount?

3. It **is easy to understand** that people today go to bed later. They
   have electrical lights, TVs, and computers in their homes.

4. **People who study the subject** have found that if you do not get
   enough sleep every night, you cannot **perform** well during the day.

5. **Unnatural** electric lighting has changed the way humans sleep.
   Humans are no longer guided by the amount of natural light.

6. **Worrying about difficulties in your life** is one thing that
   is part of the cause of insomnia, or sleeplessness.

B *Complete each sentence with your own information.*

1. _____ and _____ **contribute to** good health.

2. If I _____, this will help me **function** more effectively.

3. I _____ need to **alter** my eating habits.

4. I **consider** _____ an enjoyable way to spend my time.

Chapter 2

Write one or two complete sentences to answer each question. Use the boldfaced word or phrase in your answer.

1. How does the typical student **select** a college or university?

   _____

   _____

2. Name a **major factor** that influenced your decision to continue your education.

   _____

   _____

3. Are you **relatively** satisfied with your life? Explain why or why not.

   _____

   _____

4. **Overall**, what must a student do to achieve a college degree?

   _____

   _____

5. Think of a successful person. What **played a role** in that person's success?

   _____

   _____

6. What is one type of behavior that you **tend to** do when you are nervous?

   _____

   _____

7. Which is the most important thing to you: **a great deal of** time or a great deal of money? Explain.

   _____

   _____

Chapter 3

Complete the paragraph with words from the box.

adopted	nevertheless	status
essential	pressures	symbolize

In the article, "The Timeless Tie," the writer argues that the necktie is a useless item of clothing that exists only because of social (1) _____. According to the writer, many men must wear neckties because ties show the wearer's (2) _____ as a professional. The writer suggests that ties (3) _____ a man's desire to move up in society. Neckties were once an (4) _____ item for soldiers because they protected soldiers from bad weather, but now they are not necessary. (5) _____, men continue to wear them because they are forced by society to do so. In fact, many men around the world have (6) _____ neckties as part of their standard business clothing.

Chapter 4

A *Complete the paragraph with words from the box.*

authority	express	occasion
debate	formal	pride
dress code		

The Final Decision about the Boy's Kilt

High-school senior Nathan Warmack eventually won his case. He was permitted to wear his kilt at his (1) _____ school dance, and school superintendent Ron Anderson apologized to him. Warmack said he had wanted to wear the kilt to show his (2) _____ in his Scottish family. Anderson first stated that the school had the (3) _____ to prohibit the student from wearing the kilt under the school's (4) _____. The kilt incident sparked a strong reaction from Scottish organizations. In the end, about 12,000 people around the world signed online petitions criticizing the school's policy. After a long (5) _____, the school finally decided that the kilt was acceptable clothing for a formal (6) _____, such as a dance. One reason for the change in decision may have been an earlier U.S. Supreme Court ruling that said students have the right to freely (7) _____ their beliefs.

B *Write one or two complete sentences to answer each question. Use the boldfaced word(s) in your answer.*

1. What do you think men should wear as **appropriate** clothing at a **formal** job interview? What should women wear?

   _____

   _____

2. What kinds of clothing do you wear to **express** your personality?

   _____

   _____

3. What is something that teachers do not have the **authority** to do?

   _____

   _____

Chapter 5

A Cross out the word or phrase that is NOT close in meaning to the boldfaced word.

1. The brain **dominates** every other part of the body. It's like the central power plant of the body's machine.

   a. controls   **b.** consumes   **c.** directs

2. Our biology textbook **displays** drawings of the main parts of the brain. These illustrations help me understand the brain's workings.

   a. explains   **b.** presents   **c.** shows

3. People often **reveal** their true personalities in times of stress. In other words, stress shows us how people really are.

   a. make public   **b.** uncover   **c.** keep secret

4. Information **processing** is something that a computer—like the human brain—can do.

   a. situation   **b.** procedures   **c.** series of actions

B Write one or two complete sentences to answer each question. Use the boldfaced word in your answer.

1. How can you be more **creative** about organizing your time?

   _____

   _____

2. Are you **flexible** during your free time? Do you enjoy having no plans and just doing something unexpected?

   _____

   _____

3. Think about your best friend. Is he or she a **logical** person? Or does this person let emotions rule his or her behavior?

   _____

   _____

Chapter 6

Complete the paragraph with words from the box.

designers	enabled	extraordinary	represent
diverse	experimented	incorporated	technique

"Coco" Chanel

Gabrielle "Coco" Chanel was one of the most famous fashion
(1) _____ of the 20th century. She created a
(2) _____ range of products, from clothing and sunglasses
to perfume and jewelry. She started as a hat shop owner in Paris in
1912, and her creations sold well because they were simple yet stylish.
This experience (3) _____ her to expand into other lines of
clothing. In the 1920s, Chanel (4) _____ this simple style
into jackets, skirts, and dresses that were attractive yet comfortable.
Experts say that the secret was a special (5) _____ of
making clothing from very few pieces of fabric. Soon, the letter "C"
was used to (6) _____ all of Chanel's creations, including a
perfume, Chanel No. 5, that is still popular today. It has the number
"5" because Chanel (7) _____ with different flowers and
oils before she found the best formula. In all that she created, Coco
Chanel was indeed an (8) _____ artist.

Chapter 7

Complete the paragraph with words from the box.

aim	features	match	strategy
anticipation	involves	opposing	take advantage of

Soccer, called *football* in many countries, is the world's most popular sport. It is governed by an international group, the Fédération Internationale de Football Association. The (1) _____ of the organization is to set the rules for play. Every year, the World Cup matches occur. This championship (2) _____ a series of games between soccer teams worldwide. One by one, the teams play each other until the final (3) _____. There is great (4) _____ during the World Cup. Millions of people worldwide watch the games on television. Fans do not always act appropriately if their favorite team is losing; they may become angry at fans on the (5) _____ side. The World Cup is such an important event for soccer lovers that they are hungry for news about the game. Newspapers and TV stations explain the (6) _____ of each team and the (7) _____ of the playing fields. Advertisers (8) _____ the popularity of the sport by displaying their products on signs on the playing field or in advertisements on TV. All of these show just how popular soccer is.

Chapter 8

Complete each sentence with a word or phrase from the box.

ahead of time	concentrated	facilities	luckily
arrange	economical	in any event	site

1. I will either telephone you or email you as soon as my plane lands. _____, I will contact you to let you know we have arrived safely.

2. There are a _____ number of national parks in the southern part of Australia. With so many choices, it's hard to decide which park to visit.

3. When we travel, we prefer to _____ our hotels beforehand. That way, we don't need to find a place when we get there.

4. The weather in the city was extremely hot this summer, but _____, Eleanor avoided the heat by traveling to a cool climate.

5. Journalists visited the zoo on Friday to see the _____ of the new elephant house. Officials expect the structure to be completed by next fall.

6. Can you recommend an _____ hotel? I don't have much money, but I'd like a clean room.

7. The Museum of Art is improving its parking _____ by adding a new parking garage.

8. I hate being late to the movies! Let's get there _____ so that we have time to buy a snack.

Chapter 9

A Cross out the word or phrase that is NOT close in meaning to the boldfaced word.

1. **theory:**	guess	idea	fact	belief
2. **linked:**	caused	related	connected	tied
3. **assume:**	think	guess	know	imagine
4. **contact:**	touching	exchange	being close	communication
5. **aware of:**	know about	care about	familiar with	acquainted with
6. **roughly:**	exactly	about	more or less	approximately
7. **extent:**	degree	range	amount	importance
8. **chain:**	series	lock	sequence	progression

B Write one or two complete sentences to answer each question. Use the boldfaced word in your answer.

1. What is the difference between a **theory** and a fact?

    _____

    _____

2. Do people **assume** the best or the worst about strangers? Explain your answer.

    _____

    _____

3. Have you ever met someone through another person? Who is that **mutual** acquaintance and how did you meet him or her?

    _____

    _____

Chapter 10

A Use your dictionary to study the meanings of the words in this chart.

NOUNS	VERBS	ADJECTIVES	ADVERBS
interruption (n)	interrupt (v)	—	—
neglect (n)	neglect (v)	—	—
—	—	apparent (adj)	apparently (adv)
determination (n)	determine (v)	determined (adj)	—
willingness (n)	—	willing (adj)	willingly (adv)

B Complete the sentences with the correct word forms from Part A.

1. **interruptions / interrupted**

   In the story "Table for Two," Joseph _____ Deborah
   two times while she was reading. Both of these _____
   changed their lives.

2. **neglected / neglect**

   Joseph fell asleep on the train, and he _____ to watch
   his things. His _____ caused him to lose a book with
   Deborah's phone number.

3. **apparently / apparent**

   Joseph did not see the person who took his coat, but
   _____ it happened while he was sleeping. It's also
   _____ that the person had left the area because Joseph
   could not find any sign of his things on the train.

4. **determination / determined**

   Deborah was _____ to enjoy the sights of Paris. Such
   strong _____ enabled her to see many parts of the city
   in a short period of time.

5. **willingness / willing / willingly**

   Each time Deborah was eating in the restaurant, she
   _____ allowed a stranger to share her table. Her
   _____ to let a stranger join her led her to meet Joseph.
   Would you be _____ to permit a stranger to eat at
   your table?

Chapter 11

Read the paragraph. Write a word from the box above the boldface word or phrase with the same meaning.

analysis	crisis	load	~~reliance~~
anxiety	get ahead	pursue	struggle

Bankruptcy

In 2008, the average American had a monthly credit card debt of
about $2,000. For some, the (1) **dependence** (reliance) on credit cards becomes
so serious that they must declare themselves bankrupt. Bankruptcy
means having a heavy (2) **amount** of debt that you cannot pay
back. Bankruptcy tells the world that you're having a financial
(3) **emergency**. In an (4) **examination** of bankruptcy, however,
researchers found that bankruptcy is also a positive move because it
shows you recognize your financial problem. You reduce your level
of (5) **worry** by making a plan to repay a percentage of the money
you owe every month. It's not easy, however, because you have to
(6) **try extremely hard** over time to get back your good credit. If you
truly want to (7) **follow** your financial dreams, don't use credit cards
to **succeed** financially. Instead, save money, spend wisely, and avoid
bankruptcy.

Chapter 12

A Read each question. Circle the letter of the best answer.

1. What do you mean when you say: "I **can't beat** that store's prices"?
   a. That store has really low prices.
   b. I want to find a store with better prices.
   c. I can find better prices at other stores.

2. When a business **expands**, what does it probably need?
   a. more time
   b. more space
   c. more customers

3. If a company is **based** in a town, what does it mean?
   a. The company has customers there.
   b. The company has its main office there.
   c. The company does all its business there.

4. What is an **eager** customer most likely to do?
   a. think carefully before purchasing an item
   b. wait until the last minute to do the shopping
   c. arrive at the store and wait until it opens

5. Joe **stimulated** the local economy. What did he do?
   a. He spent more money.
   b. He didn't spend any money.
   c. He moved to a new city.

6. Shopping centers sometimes provide **exhibitions** to attract customers. What is one example?
   a. a big sale
   b. an art show
   c. a famous person

7. What does this description tell you: "The young man's clothing was **coordinated**"?
   a. The man wore clothing that looked expensive.
   b. The man did not take time to choose his clothes carefully.
   c. The colors and styles of the man's clothes matched well.

Chapter 13

Read each phrase. Check (✔) to show whether the boldfaced word is used as a noun, verb, adjective, or adverb.

	NOUN	VERB	ADJECTIVE	ADVERB
1. promotion				
a. a **promotion** at work				
b. to **promote** a worker				
2. permanent				
a. a **permanent** increase				
b. to close **permanently**				
3. adapt				
a. to **adapt** to a new city				
b. a difficult **adaptation**				
4. motivator				
a. a strong **motivator**				
b. to **motivate** me to study				
5. stable				
a. a **stable** job				
b. job **stability**				
6. retain				
a. to **retain** information				
b. the **retention** of information				

Chapter 14

Read each question. Circle the letter of the best answer.

1. What do you say to a friend who is wearing **fashionable** clothes?
   a. "That outfit is really unattractive."
   b. "You are really in style!"
   c. "My grandmother had a dress like that."

2. Which statement best expresses this idea: "**Chances are,** it's going to rain"?
   a. It's likely to rain.
   b. There's a small chance of rain.
   c. I'm not certain whether it will rain.

3. What are you looking for if you are looking for the **roots** of a problem?
   a. its results
   b. its causes
   c. its solutions

4. What do you do when you **cite** a piece of information?
   a. You remember it.
   b. You refer to it.
   c. You look it up.

5. If there is a high **incidence** of crime in your neighborhood, what does it mean?
   a. Most crimes occur at night.
   b. There are few crimes.
   c. There are many crimes.

6. Which of these actions describes a friend that you can **count on**?
   a. The friend always borrows money from you.
   b. The friend always acts politely to you.
   c. The friend always keeps his or her promises.

7. Which of the following are generally NOT **statistics**?
   a. numbers
   b. opinions
   c. percentages

Chapter 15

Read each question. Circle the letter of the best answer.

1. If someone looks **as if** she is sick, how does she look?
   a. ill
   b. normal
   c. healthy

2. Which statement best expresses this idea: "I'm **quite** happy with my new job"?
   a. I'm not happy.
   b. I'm somewhat happy.
   c. I'm extremely happy.

3. If you feel like you **swallowed** a piece of sunshine, how would you feel?
   a. terrible
   b. wonderful
   c. very full

4. If you smile **charmingly,** how will people react?
   a. They will want to meet you.
   b. They will not notice you.
   c. They will stay away from you.

5. Which statement best expresses this idea: "This person is a **jewel**"?
   a. This person is rich.
   b. This person is cold.
   c. This person is special.

6. If you understand basic mathematics, but nothing **beyond** that, how much mathematics do you know?
   a. only basic mathematics
   b. many types of mathematics
   c. only certain types of mathematics

7. John smiled secretively, and his friends wondered what was **behind** John's smile. What were the friends thinking?
   a. Why is John sad?
   b. Why is John smiling?
   c. Why doesn't John smile more?

Chapter 16

Mark the statements T (true) or F (false).

_____ 1. When students show their **enthusiasm** for a subject, they are bored by the subject.

_____ 2. You act **coolly** towards a person if you do not like that person.

_____ 3. There was plenty of food, good conversation, and dancing. The party was **delightful**.

_____ 4. If good friends want to talk, they should sit **side by side** on the same bench.

_____ 5. If you **dislike** food at a restaurant, you should ask the waiter to bring you something else to eat.

_____ 6. People sometimes show their **rudeness** in stores by smiling and speaking politely to clerks.

_____ 7. A **lovely** smile can brighten up someone's day.

_____ 8. If you are **pleased** with a gift, you don't like it and you return it to the store.

Target Vocabulary

*Coxhead's *Academic Word List* (2000)
**Dilin Liu's *The Most Frequently Used American English Idioms* (2003)

UNIT 1
(Chapters 1 & 2)

a great deal
alter*
artificial
consider
contribute to
factor*
function*
major*
makes sense**
overall
play a role in
relatively
researchers*
select
stress
tend to

UNIT 2
(Chapters 3 & 4)

adopted
appropriate*
authority*
comment*
consequently*
debate*
dress code
due to
essential
express

formal
get rid of**
nevertheless*
occasion
pressure
pride
status*
struggled
symbolize*
universal

UNIT 3
(Chapters 5 & 6)

creative*
decades*
designers*
displayed
diverse*
dominate
enabled
experimented
extraordinary
flexibility*
incorporated*
indicated*
logical*
otherwise
processing*
represents
revealed*
technique*

UNIT 4
(Chapters 7 & 8)

ahead of time
aim
anticipation*
arrange
companions
concentrated
economical
element*
environment*
facilities*
features
in any event
involves*
luckily
match
opposing
site*
strategy*
take advantage of**

UNIT 5
(Chapters 9 & 10)

am aware of*
apparently*
are willing to
assume*
barely
chain
contact*

deserted
determined
edge
entirely
extent
interrupted
linked to*
mutual*
neglected
roughly
theory*
throughout

UNIT 6
(Chapters 11 & 12)

analysis
anxiety
based
beat
cleverly
consumers*
crisis
eager
engage
exhibitions*

expand
generation*
get ahead
load
previous
pursue*
reliance on*
stimulated
struggling
wander

UNIT 7
(Chapters 13 & 14)

accommodate*
adapt*
arrangement
chances are
cite*
count on
eventually
fashionable
incidence
motivator
permanent
promotion

retain
roots
stable
statistics
sticks with
transition

UNIT 8
(Chapters 15 & 16)

a find
as if**
behind
beyond
charmingly
coolly
delightful
disliked
enthusiasm
jewel
lovely
pleased
quite
rudeness
side by side
swallowed

Credits

Photo Credits: Cover: Cloud Nine Productions/Corbis; **Page 1** Shutterstock; **Page 2** © The Metropolitan Museum of Art / Art Resource, NY; **Page 11** © Alex Bruno; **Page 21** Bigstockphoto; **Page 22** iStockphoto; **Page 28** © picturescolourlibrary.com; **Page 33** iStockphoto; **Page 43** left Shutterstock, right iStockphoto; **Page 44** Shutterstock; **Page 56** © 1960 Eames Office, LLC (eamesoffice.com); **Page 58** © 1954 Eames Office, LLC (eamesoffice.com), from the Collections of the Library of Congress, The Work of Charles and Ray Eames; **Page 67** left Shutterstock, right Shutterstock; **Page 68** © Peter Dazeley/Getty Images; **Page 80** Photolibrary.com; **Page 91** Shutterstock; **Page 92** top left iStockphoto, bottom left iStockphoto, top right Shutterstock, bottom right Shutterstock; **Page 104** © Lambert/Getty Images; **Page 115** Shutterstock; **Page 116** Shutterstock; **Page 129** © Michael Newman/Photo Edit; **Page 137** Shutterstock; **Page 138** Shutterstock; **Page 149** Shutterstock; **Page 161** Shutterstock; **Page 164** © Getty Images.

Text Credits: Page 35 *A Young Man and His Kilt*—Reprinted with permission of The Associated Press, November 9, 2006.

Page 106 *Table for Two*—Excerpt "Table for Two" by Lori Peikoff. I Thought My Father Was Good, edited by Paul Auster. Copyright © 2002 by Paul Auster. Published by Picador. Reprinted with permission of the Carol Mann Agency.

Page 152 *Staying Home with Mama*—From Newsweek, 8/14/2000, © 2000 Newsweek, Inc. All rights reserved. Used by permission and protected by the Copyright Laws of the United States. The printing, copying, redistribution, or retransmission of the Material without express written permission is prohibited.

Pages 164, 176 *Bliss*—Excerpt from "The Doll's House and Other Stories" by Katherine Mansfield from Penguin Readers. www.penguinreaders.com. Copyright © 2008. Published by Pearson Education Limited. Reprinted with permission.

Index